HOW DO YOU LIGHT A FART?

HOW DO YOU LIGHT A FART?

And 150 Other Essential Things Every Guy Should Know about Science

BOBBY MERCER

A adamsmedia
AVON, MASSACHUSETTS

Published by
Adams Media, a division of F+W Media, Inc.
57 Littlefield Street, Avon, MA 02322. U.S.A.
www.adamsmedia.com

ISBN 10: 1-59869-984-9
ISBN 13: 978-1-59869-984-5

Printed in the United States of America.

J I H G F E D C B A

Library of Congress Cataloging-in-Publication Data
is available from the publisher.

Illustrations on pages 124 and 153 © Neubau Welt
(*www.NeubauWelt.com*)

This book is available at quantity discounts for bulk purchases.
For information, please call 1-800-289-0963.

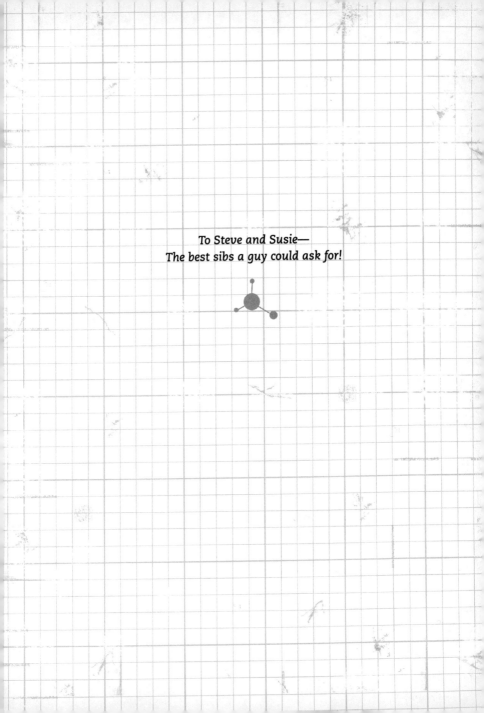

To Steve and Susie—
The best sibs a guy could ask for!

CONTENTS

ACKNOWLEDGMENTS

Books don't happen without the support of many people. I have the deepest appreciation for all of the people that helped and listened. I owe a special debt to Matt Kissling for always being there when I needed a friend. I also want to thank my Dad, Buzz Mercer, for teaching me about power tools, WD-40, and how to catch a baseball. I want to thank my Mom, Joyce Mercer, for always believing in Susie, Steve, and me.

I wish to thank my agent, Kathy Green, for her help, guidance, and championing of this book. In my opinion, she is the best in the business. I want to thank Andrea Norville, Katie Corcoran Lytle, and the wonderful people at Adams Media for believing in this book and lending their expertise.

I want to thank all of my great friends for listening and offering anecdotes. Thanks to Jeff Andrews, Scott Buchanan, David Burdette, Rich Canamucio, Richard and Nancy Canamucio, Dana Conner, Matt Daigle, Mike Flowe, Richard Gabriel, Mike Garity, Kim Kessler, Laura Laughter, Ann and Mitch Leonard, Charlie Metcalf, Joe Potter, Courtney Ross, Marvin Smith, Bobby Somerville, Jenny Thomas, and Bill Van Cleve.

The biggest debt of gratitude goes to my wonderful wife, Michele. Thanks for being my best friend and believing in me.

INTRODUCTION

Science has changed our lives for the better and will continue to do so. The advances of the past one hundred years boggle the mind. Things that were once unimaginable—surround sound, cell phones, duct tape, and WD-40—are now indispensable in our daily lives.

Science was the first academic pursuit in our life. As youngsters we saw new things and wondered why? Hopefully, you still wonder why when you see something new. The process of examining the world around us *is* science. And science (like all things) is easier to understand when it is mixed with a little humor.

In the last few years, several things have become clear to me. One, learning needs to be fun, whether you are eight or eighty. Almost all public speakers break the ice with a joke before they push their agenda, because you learn better when you are laughing. Two, we need to embrace our manliness. Be glad that men and women are different. We have a different language than women. We say sweat, she says perspire. Guys need textbooks written in their language. I love science and being a guy, so combining the two seemed like a perfect idea—a science textbook written for the male of the species. This book is designed to educate and amuse. And the best part is . . . you won't have to take a final exam when you finish reading it.

Guys are different in the humor department also. We see humor where most women never would. We smile when our dog moves to the other side of the room after polluting our air with noxious fumes. We make jokes about erectile dysfunction medications (at least until we need them). We smile as we ponder what life was like before the remote control was invented. We laugh about butt gas, burnt knuckle hair, and women.

You will learn about all sorts of manly things in the following pages. Serious science is mixed with a dose of humor. This book will teach you the science of flatulence, neat bar tricks, and why three-piece balls are better for golf. You will also be taught why space explosions are better in the movie theater and at least three ways to open a locked door.

That leads me to this public service announcement about this book. Cherish it forever and buy copies for all of your law-abiding friends. In your will, leave instructions for it to be given to a charity. But NEVER donate it to any books-for-prisoners charity. Also never give this book as a breakup present to your soon-to-be ex-girlfriend.

Now that you've been forewarned, sit down and hang on as we examine the science of being a guy.

ONE: THINGS THAT GO BOOM

Men love explosions, and our collective fascination with fire and explosions is something inherently male. Hollywood has recognized and catered to that male lust for years with a plethora of action films every summer. In the real world cars almost never explode on impact, but every stunt car crash is accompanied by a raging fireball that stretches a thousand feet into the air. The film industry spends millions of dollars to get our butts into the seats with tons of high-tech pyrotechnics because they know the secret to cinematic success: Men will gladly fork over their money to watch great explosions. The movie can even suck, but most men will still leave the theater happy if there are jaw-dropping explosions.

Grill manufacturers have also learned this secret to success. One of the reasons guys love cooking on a charcoal grill is because of the fun—and danger—that comes from lighting it. Throwing a match onto a pile of gas-laden charcoal briquettes is the highlight of many picnics. Most guys would never wax any part of their body, but we'll gladly risk burning off our facial hair for the thrill of that momentarily out-of-control flame. The wonderful whoosh sound and the immediate six-foot-high wall of flame have signified the beginning of many glorious testosterone-filled hours spent standing happily over the grill. The chance that we may lose our eyebrows is only an added bonus. So light a fire, say goodbye to your body hair, and put on your flameproof suit as we examine the world of pyrotechnics.

Scientifically Speaking

Men love to wonder and that is the nature of science.

—Ralph Waldo Emerson

HOW DO FIRECRACKERS EXPLODE?

Men have loved firecrackers ever since the first time we saw one explode. It's safe to say that the male penchant for going overboard led to the rise of the pack of firecrackers, because if firecrackers are fun, packs are fun squared. The added fact that firecrackers are illegal in many states only adds to the allure, and a chance to bend the rules and get a giant explosion is impossible to pass up.

A firecracker is a tube of paper wrapped several times for strength and sealed at both ends with clay or plastic. Flash powder is in the center, and a fuse goes through one end to ignite it. The fuse will burn into the flash powder, causing it to explode. The rapid explosion causes the casing to crack open with a loud pop. In a pack of firecrackers a longer fuse runs down the center, which causes all of the individual fuses to ignite in rapid succession. For your safety, only buy approved firecrackers and use approved practices.

Brain Fart

Firecrackers are legal in some states in the Deep South; moonshine, firecrackers, and red clay roads just seem to go together.

HOW IS DYNAMITE MADE SAFE FOR EXPLOSIONS?

The familiar red cylinder with the long fuse is a television prop. These sticks have been a Hollywood staple for years, but in reality, dynamite can be molded into any shape. Dynamite is nitroglycerin (a liquid) that is mixed with some absorbent base material to make it safer to transport and use. A more sensitive explosive is usually housed in one end of the dynamite and is used to ignite the nitroglycerin-soaked materials. An electric blasting cap ignites this sensitive explosive, and the resulting small explosion causes the dynamite to detonate. In the early days, the blasting cap was similar to a firecracker, but almost all are electronic nowadays. Push a button, complete the electric circuit, and boom!

As many people know, dynamite was invented by Alfred Nobel, the same Nobel of the prizes awarded in physics, chemistry, medicine, literature, and peace. It is commonly believed that he left his fortune to create the prizes after reading his own premature obituary that called him "a merchant of death" for his invention of dynamite. (You know you're having a bad day when your own obit is in the paper.) Nobel then changed his legacy by leaving a vast sum of money to start awarding the prizes. He also left a few pissed-off relatives.

Scientifically Speaking

A little knowledge is a dangerous thing. So is a lot.

—Albert Einstein

HOW IS AN AERIAL FIREWORK DISPLAY MADE?

Gigantic firework displays explode in all manners of colors, drawing cheers from anyone watching. It will often take days for pyrotechnical experts to set up for that twenty-minute display. Let's peek inside an individual shell to see how it works.

The outside part of a firework shell is usually formed from paper or thin cardboard. Running down the center of the shell is a large firecracker-like bursting charge. Surrounding the center is black powder, often mixed in with pieces of aluminum, steel, iron, zinc, or magnesium that create shiny sparks as they burn. The shells also contain stars—sparkler-like devices that account for the falling light trails we see. Different chemicals are added to the stars to create the colors as they burn. You may have learned the secret to colors in a chemistry class; all elements burn with a characteristic flame color. Common elements used in fireworks are strontium for red, barium for green, copper for blue, magnesium for white, and sodium for yellow. The way the stars are packed in the shell accounts for the different shapes when the fireworks explode. Ovals, circles, and palm trees are all created by positioning the stars certain distances away from the bursting charge. Some shells also have smaller individual shells inside that explode as they fall to create even more patterns.

Shells are fired out of a mortar by the use of a lifting charge. The lifting charge lifts the firework into the air and also ignites a fuse that explodes the bursting charge at a certain height. A show may have hundreds of different mortars all set to be launched in a particular order. Home aerial displays can also be purchased legally in some states (mostly in the South). The shells are smaller, but the science is the same.

Basic Firework Design

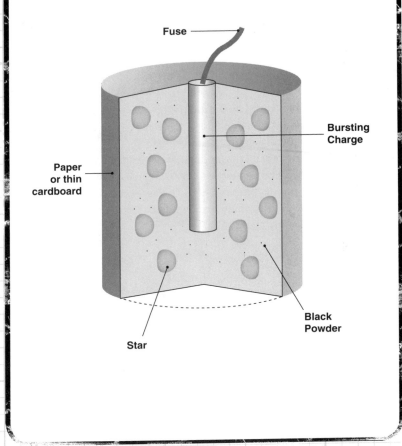

Fuse

Bursting Charge

Paper or thin cardboard

Black Powder

Star

WHAT IS THE DIFFERENCE BETWEEN DYNAMITE AND TNT?

Contrary to popular belief, dynamite and TNT are not the same thing. Whereas dynamite is nitroglycerin-soaked sawdust, TNT is a specific chemical compound. *TNT* is much easier to spell than *trinitrotoluene* (and *dynamite*), so it is perfect for cartoons and action movies. It is a yellow crystal that was originally used as a yellow dye, but once men realized the dye exploded they found uses that were a little more fun. TNT is extremely stable and very hard to detonate, but when it does, any men standing around cheer.

Did You Know?

TNT was originally used as a yellow clothing dye.

TNT can be bought in blocks by itself, but it is more commonly combined with other materials to form an even stronger explosive sold only to professionals. This is a good thing because, given the chance, many men would buy it simply to liven up a Fourth of July picnic.

HOW DOES A LARGE BUILDING IMPLODE INTO A NEAT PILE OF RUBBLE?

Bringing down a twenty-story building takes the utmost care, a ton of scientific know-how, and a few hundred pounds of explosives. Building implosions are small, controlled explosions designed to bring a building down on its footprint. Blasters spend years perfecting their craft, and most implosions worldwide are handled by the same few companies. But let's face it; these blasters probably grew up stuffing firecrackers in mailboxes, and now it's their full-time job, only the firecrackers are just larger.

Often blasters will use plastic explosives rather than TNT or dynamite. C-4 and Semtex are two of the better-known types of plastic explosives. They are both formed by mixing an explosive powder with a plastic binding agent to make it less volatile. The plastic also allows the explosive to be shaped any way you want. It can be thought of as modeling clay for pyros. You could make all of these cute little statues that would blow up with a good whack. Demolition experts pack the explosive into cracks in walls that need to come down. They also use it to cut through steel I-beams when bringing down buildings.

The blocks of plastic explosives will only explode with a large shock, usually from a blasting cap. Without this large shock you can actually light them on fire without an explosion. Supposedly you can even shoot a block of plastic explosives and not have it blow up. I think I am just going to trust that fact.

It can take engineers up to three or four months to prepare a building for a three- or four-second collapse. They study the blueprints (if available) to locate load-bearing columns, which are then rigged with explosives and wrapped with fabric to contain the explosion. Other non-load-bearing walls on that particular floor are removed. All of the charges are set to fire in a particular order by using electronic blasting caps—small, electronically operated firecrackers—to begin the explosion of the charge. Interior columns are detonated first to start the building falling inward. A few dozen more explosions and the building becomes a heap of rubble. The outside of the building may also be wrapped in chainlink fence or fabric to contain the total explosion. Other buildings in the area are also protected.

Many companies still use the old, easily recognizable T-handle plunger that is pressed down to start the implosion; it just makes for better publicity pictures. The plunger sends an electric charge to the blasting caps and the building starts to fall.

Some companies use the remotes seen in newer movies. These new remotes look like our favorite—the television remote. In the high-tech world we live in, some implosions are even started by hitting the Enter key. A computer then controls the firing sequence.

No matter what else is going on, safety is always the number one concern for the blasters. They announce the demolition to all the local news stations for safety and to ensure a big crowd. This gigantic crash is sure to be filmed for the six o'clock news (or maybe for a movie) and will attract a lot of spectators. However, even though getting paid to play with explosives could be a lot of fun, remember the danger and don't forget to wear your hard hat!

HOW DO HAND GRENADES WORK?

One of the earlier forms of explosives in battle was the hand grenade. Grenades are just gigantic firecrackers designed to injure, maim, or disorient. The term *grenade* actually comes from the word *pomegranate*, since the shrapnel reminded people of those wonderful, sweet seeds. Over 1,000 years ago, combatants filled canisters with explosives and any metal they had lying around to create grenades. Grenades have come a long way since then and now come in many different varieties.

Mention "grenade" and most people envision what are known as fragmentation grenades. In a fragmentation grenade, a hard plastic or metal shell surrounds an explosive and a percussion cap. A pin is inserted to keep the grenade safe. When the pin is pulled, you are still safe as long as you squeeze the safety handle. When the grenade is thrown, the handle flies off and the timer starts. Most grenades will explode two to six seconds after the handle is released. Upon explosion, the casing shreds into tiny pieces creating shrapnel that can injure and maim.

Grenades have been developed for all sorts of specialized uses over the last one hundred years. Smoke and tear gas have both been added to grenades. Smoke grenades create thick, dense smoke used to signal a location or give people something to hide behind. Tear gas grenades are designed to fill an enclosed space with tear gas or to create a barrier in front of a rioting crowd.

Several grenades, primarily designed not to kill, have been developed for the police. These include the stun and the sting grenade. Stun grenades, called flashbangs by police, create a tremendous amount of light and a deafening noise. Both of these will combine to completely disorient an unsuspecting person for up to five seconds. Sting grenades have two rubber shells with tiny superballs placed between the two shells. When they explode, the area is covered with stinging pellets.

Some grenades are designed to explode on impact instead of using a timed fuse, which limits the ability of an enemy to throw them back. These grenades are safe until activated. Today many grenades are launched instead of thrown. Now you don't have to be a professional baseball pitcher to heave them a long way. Pull the trigger and away they go. After they leave the barrel of the launcher, stabilizing fins come out and the fuse is activated. They will explode on contact. The U.S. Army even developed a machine gun that fires 400 grenade rounds a minute.

Grenades are currently being developed that will explode a certain distance away from the gun. This will give troops the ability to injure a person standing behind a barricade.

Did You Know?

The Hand Grenade is a trademarked drink that first appeared in New Orleans in 1984. The ingredient list is a closely guarded secret. It is marketed as the strongest drink on Bourbon Street.

HOW DO YOU MAKE BUTANE LIGHTERS EXPLODE?

Try this out on used-up disposable butane lighters. Use the lighter for any and all variety of pyrotechnic pursuits until it's empty. Then stand twenty-five or thirty feet away from a concrete wall and heave the lighter as hard as you can. Upon hitting the wall, some lighters will create a loud pop along with a mini-burst of flame. Some probably won't, and you could look really stupid in front of your friends. For safety reasons, you and your friends should keep a good distance away from the wall.

Did You Know?

Butane lighters won't light when they are extremely cold. The butane won't vaporize easily at low temperatures.

Why does this work? Even after it is supposedly empty, the lighter still contains trace amounts of butane. The lighter will break open when it hits the wall, and you also may get a spark. Put the little amount of butane together with that spark and you get a pop. NEVER try this with a full lighter. It's not supposed to work when a lighter is full because the vapor ignites better than the liquid, but it is not worth the chance.

HOW DO YOU START A FIRE IN THE WOODS?

Friction creates heat. Think about rubbing your hands together on a cold day. Rubbing two sticks together can work the same way to create heat, and if you're very lucky (and can rub incredibly fast) you may get a fire. You can also make a bow using string on a stick. Wrap the string around another stick and place the end of this stick on a piece of wood surrounded by dry brush. Then just play the bow like a violinist. With any luck, the friction will eventually light the dry brush.

Obviously, a far better way to start a fire in the woods is to use matches. My motto is "If you go camping, take matches." As an adult, camping trips often mean romance, and you don't want to wear yourself out rubbing sticks. The stick trick is cute and may get you a merit badge, but matches will get you on your way to a romantic fire quicker. Five gallons of gas, or an entire bottle of lighter fluid, will help you even more in your quest for fire. But be careful; you'll lose any chance for romance if you burn the tent down.

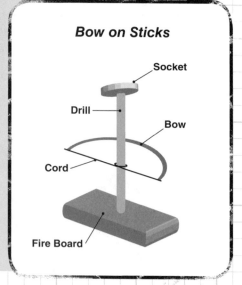

Bow on Sticks

Socket

Drill

Bow

Cord

Fire Board

HOW DOES HOLLYWOOD CREATE CAR CRASHES?

Push an abandoned car off a cliff and you get a twisted hunk of steel. Turn on a movie camera and repeat, and the car will mysteriously burst into flames. Filmmakers have known this secret for years. All of their car crashes involve giant fireballs. My favorite car crashes involve a car going off a cliff and actually igniting on the way down. In real life, a car landing after a fall has maybe a one in a million chance of catching fire. That's because liquid gas doesn't explode very well; it just burns. Gasoline vapor is what causes explosions, and you need a lot of it. Gasoline in a car tank is in liquid form, and not much vapor escapes.

To get the explosions we're used to seeing on screen, stunt coordinators load a car full of fireworks designed to explode at the director's cue. They have the ultimate pyromaniac dream job; they play with fire for a living, and the bigger the inferno the better.

Brain Fart

Let's face it: Men love giant explosions. We even love explosions that we know could never happen as long as they are accompanied by movie popcorn or Milk Duds.

HOW DO SPACESHIPS EXPLODE?

Giant explosions happen in space all the time. They happen even more when you add actors, directors, and special-effects people. Watching the Death Star explode still makes people cheer. However, the giant seat-shaking explosion of the Death Star has many of the same flaws as all sci-fi movie explosions, such as the deafening sound and the size of the fireball. Many people mistakenly assume you can't have an explosion without oxygen, but explosions in space are common—and often accompanied by giant fireballs. Most explosions require an oxidizer like oxygen, but most rockets carry an oxidizer for their fuel supply, so they could explode. The size of the explosion would be limited by the lack of oxygen in space, but an explosion would still take place. And without air pressure around, the pieces would fly off pretty fast.

The big problem with movie space explosions is sound. The explosion could create radio waves that could be picked up by a radio, but there wouldn't be conventional sound waves. Sound is a mechanical wave, which means it requires a medium such as water, steel, air, or any other form of matter. But space is almost a perfect vacuum and lacks one important thing for the sound wave to propagate—matter. There are a few random molecules every few thousand cubic miles, but not enough to collide and carry the sound. Of course, to hear explosions you would have to take your helmet off. Bad idea! Rule number one in space—leave your helmet on.

Scientifically Speaking

The scientific theory I like best is that the rings of Saturn are composed entirely of lost airline luggage.

—Mark Russell

CAN A FLAME BE ROUND?

Whether we're cuddling by a romantic fireplace, celebrating a birthday, or roasting marshmallows at a bonfire, flames of all size amaze us. Fire is a byproduct of a chemical reaction of oxygen and some manner of fuel. Gas, wood, and your sister's ponytail will all burn if they get hot enough.

Flames rise and are pointed because the hot gases in the flame are less dense than the surrounding air and the smoke rises. The heavier, dense air is pulled down by the Earth's gravitational field. Also, different colors indicate different amounts of heat. The hottest parts are blue, while the cooler sections are orange. Don't believe me? Touch them and find out (just kidding!).

Flames lit in space could actually be spherical but only in the presence of microgravity. Microgravity is what we often call weightlessness. Contrary to popular belief, astronauts in space are not weightless. They have the same amount of weight they have on Earth and are being pulled toward the nearest gravitational field. For shuttle astronauts, this is the Earth. The shuttle is also being pulled down at the same rate, so the astronaut and shuttle fall together. The astronauts don't push on the shuttle, so they feel weightless.

Microgravity works the same way on flames lit in space. Without the effects of gravity to pull down the dense air, the flame will be round. The smoke "rises" in all directions instead of just one. I can tell you right now that if I ever get a shuttle ride, I am going to light a match.

Did You Know?

If you want to get taller as an adult, all you have to do is go to space. Without gravity to pull you down, your spine will decompress and you'll grow by up to two inches.

ARE SAFETY MATCHES REALLY SAFE?

Good old safety matches are designed to ignite only by using a striker board attached to the pack. Striker boards were actually placed inside the cover of the first matchbooks, which caused the entire pack to ignite. Today the striker board is on the outside of the pack. The head of the safety match usually contains potassium chlorate mixed with sulfur, a binder, and glass powder. The striker board contains red phosphorus, a binder, and powdered glass. Rubbing the match across the striker creates heat because of friction. When you strike a match, a tiny amount of the red phosphorus becomes white phosphorus, which ignites easily with the heat created. This sets offs a decomposition of the potassium chlorate to release oxygen. The sulfur ignites and burns the wooden stick or cardboard strip.

Strike-anywhere matches are hard to find because they are more dangerous. These matches have a different colored head that contains phosphorus sulfide, potassium chlorate, binders, and glass. The phosphorus sulfide ignites easily, and the potassium chlorate releases oxygen, which causes the match to burn brighter. The stick will also burn to give you a longer flame. Strike-anywhere matches are misnamed. They don't actually light anywhere, so they should probably be called strike-almost-anywhere-that-is-rough-and-dry matches. You can't light one in a swimming pool or on a dinner plate, but zippers, old jeans, and the bottom of your shoe all work. I've never tried my zipper; there are parts of my body that are scared of fire.

Did You Know?

Not all wood burns. The bark of a giant redwood tree is actually fireproof. An occasional fire is good for a redwood forest because it will clear out much of the undergrowth that drinks the water that the redwood needs to survive.

HOW DO THEY PUT THE "POP" IN POP ROCKS?

This pop-in-your-mouth candy is unique and fun to eat. The candy is created using high-pressure carbon dioxide similar to what you find in soda. The ingredients for Pop Rocks are melted, the carbon dioxide is added, and the concoction is allowed to cool. During cooling, tiny carbon dioxide bubbles are trapped in the candy. As the candy comes into contact with the hot saliva in your mouth, it melts, the bubbles pop open, and you get that crazy feeling on your tongue.

The candy also gave rise to one of the most enduring urban myths ever—that drinking a cola and eating Pop Rocks would cause your stomach to explode. For this reason, sales dropped and General Foods actually stopped selling the candy, even selling the rights and formula. Luckily, a new company brought the candy back for a whole new generation of kids.

A neat trick is to place a few Pop Rocks on your tongue and try to hold them against the roof of your mouth. Try not to do this while your coworkers are watching. They will laugh, and you won't. Just don't wash the remnants down with a cold soda . . .

Scientifically Speaking

If you can see light at the end of the tunnel, you are looking the wrong way.

—Barry Commoner

HOW DO YOU MAKE
LIFE SAVERS SPARK?

When chewed in a dark room, Wintergreen Life Savers create an interesting phenomenon: They make your mouth glow blue! Try it for yourself. Go into a bathroom, turn off the lights, let your eyes adjust, and crunch away. You get tiny bolts of lightning.

The light is due to a process called triboluminescence. It comes from the electrons that are ripped free as you chew the candy. These electrons combine with nitrogen molecules to produce light. Normally this is light you couldn't see, but the oil of wintergreen is fluorescent, which helps the process along. The fluorescent oil absorbs short-wavelength light (that we can't see) and emits longer-wavelength visible light. Your mouth glows!

Remember, the light created through this process is very faint, so don't throw out your flashlights and buy cases of candy just yet. However, in a pinch you could buy a bottle of the flavoring, swig a little, and eat your Halloween candy to light your way home. Wait! What do you mean you don't still go door-to-door for trick or treating?

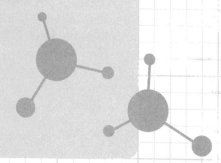

WHAT IS THE "TRICK" TO A TRICK CANDLE?

A normal candle is composed of two parts: paraffin wax and a wick. Paraffin wax is a thick hydrocarbon that comes from crude oil. The wick is an absorbent material that pulls up the melted liquid wax. The flame melts the wax, and the liquid goes up the wick and vaporizes. The paraffin vapor is what burns.

When you blow out a candle, a smoldering ember continues to vaporize some wax, but it isn't hot enough to ignite the vapor. A trick candle has an additional material, usually magnesium, in the wick that ignites at a very low temperature. The ember lights the magnesium particles, the paraffin vapor reignites, and the candle flame is reborn.

These magic relighting candles are perfect for office celebrations, kids' parties, and anyone who really believes their wishes will come true after blowing out the candle. As a kid, I kept wishing to be six-foot-five inches to help my football career; that didn't work out. I also wasted several birthdays wishing for a Corvette. No 'Vette, but I do love my minivan. Most people would be better off just wishing for a piece of cake. Even with a trick candle your wish would come true.

> **Did You Know?**
>
> Aluminum, iron, zinc, steel, and magnesium can all be used in sparklers to create the sparkle.

HOW DO YOUR FEET NOT BURN WHILE FIREWALKING?

Walking across fire is associated with islands in the South Pacific, girls in grass skirts, umbrella drinks, and coconuts. I just associate firewalking with a single word—NUTS. I originally thought you had to be somewhat crazy—or liquored up—to think this is a good idea, but as I studied it, I realize these guys are experts in science. Firewalking is actually a rite of passage, a healing ritual, and a test of faith for many cultures.

Firewalking is most often done over a bed of glowing embers, and the science is fascinating. When hot and cold objects come together, the hot one loses heat to the cold object due primarily to molecules colliding at the surface. If they stay together long enough, they'll reach the same temperature. How fast they reach this equilibrium temperature depends upon specific heat capacity, mass, and thermal conductivity for each object. The product of mass and specific heat capacity for any object is called heat capacity. Energy is conserved, so the heat capacity lost by the coals is equal to the heat capacity gained by the feet.

The final temperature will end up closer to the initial temperature of the feet for several reasons. One, our bodies (and our feet) contain water. Water has a high specific heat capacity, and the coals have a low specific heat capacity. This causes the foot temperature to rise only a small amount. Second, the thermal conductivity of water is high. This spreads the heat

> ## Brain Fart
>
> Firewalking should never be done while wearing a grass skirt.

throughout your body quickly so your soles don't burn (as long as you keep moving). The conductivity of the coals is very low, so heat from other parts of the coals can't get to the top very easily. The coals are also covered in ash, which has an even lower rate of thermal conductivity. Third, the coals are uneven, so not very much of your foot has to be in contact with the coal at any time.

Never try firewalking at home. There are a few musts that have to be taken into account: The coals must burn a long time to completely remove any water, and never under any circumstances should you stop in the middle. Fill up on umbrella drinks and get across the coals as fast as possible. Afterwards, go chase the girls with the grass skirts.

HOW DO YOU BREATHE FIRE?

There is no more spectacular stunt than breathing fire. A quick swig of fuel and the performer blows out a tremendous fireball. This is not a do-it-yourself gig. Let me see, a flaming torch and a mouthful of fuel—both of these make me think danger. They also make me think of impaired reasoning abilities.

The science is pretty straightforward. Take a mouthful of fuel and blow it across a lit torch. Fire needs three things: fuel, oxygen, and flame. The fuels can vary, but kerosene and lamp oil are the two most common. The torches are usually homemade by the performers. The breathers also must take into account nearby objects, wind speed, and wind direction. The fuel must be blown at an angle between 45 and 75 degrees to minimize danger. Too low and their arm might be smoking. Too high and burning fuel might rain down on them.

> **Did You Know?**
>
> If you prefer to drink your fire, try a Flaming B52 or a Serbian Guerilla Fighter. Looking for something more familiar? Visit your local Chinese restaurant for the ever-popular Scorpion Bowl. Just be sure to blow out the flame before drinking!

Blowback is the most dangerous aspect of breathing fire. Blowback is when the flame follows the fuel back to the mouth. Most of the fuels are carcinogenic at best and fatal if swallowed at worst. Dragons (as some like to be called) usually have a trained safety expert nearby with an extinguisher and a wet fire blanket in case something goes wrong.

As guys, we may love hot and spicy things, but breathing fire is best left to the trained professionals. If you really have a desire to breathe fire, head over to your favorite wing place and chow down. Try this for fun. Eat the hottest wings listed on the menu. Immediately follow the wings with an entire jalapeño pepper and chase with a bottle of your favorite hot sauce. This concoction is guaranteed to make your eyeballs sweat. Personally, my favorite hot and spicy things are female.

TWO: REV YOUR ENGINES

For men, the need for speed is as basic as life itself. The first caveman that walked the earth learned that speed was the secret to staying alive. He had to be able to outrun the saber-toothed tiger to see the light of the next day. Well actually, he just had to outrun one fellow caveperson to survive. The first race was born, and we've been racing ever since.

The occasional state trooper is just part of the game. Guys simply like to compete. Educational experts have said that competition hurts self-esteem, but these experts are just mad because they never won anything. Even visiting relatives can be turned into a race by challenging family members to set record times on the trips between cities. My brother-in-law and I look for any advantage to shave a few minutes off our time. I would easily win if I could just get my entire family to wear diapers.

Racing technology has grown from racing on the beach to today's super speedways, and whether it's NASCAR, Formula 1, drag racing, motorcycle racing, the Tour de France, or even lawn mowers, guys love a good race. And racing involves science. So strap in and hold on as we examine the world of racing.

WHY DON'T RACECAR TIRES HAVE TREADS?

Dragsters, NASCAR cars, and racing bikes are all made without treads. Tread helps a car maintain traction (grip) with the road surface in wet weather and when turning. Passenger car tires come with treads for that reason, and that's why most races are delayed by the slightest hint of rain.

Tires are the most important part of a racecar because they are the only part in contact with the road. Normal car tires are hard, which helps them last longer, but racecar tires are soft. The soft rubber uses adhesion to increase traction. Walk on a racetrack and you will see thousands of rubber marbles at the bottom of the banked track. These rubber marbles come from tire erosion and form little balls that roll to the bottom. Racecar tires are also wider, which gives the driver even more grip since more rubber adheres to the road. The grip of the tires is what helps the cars turn the corners.

Racecar tires are designed to be driven only a few hundred miles and are specially designed for each track. The tires are even designed for each side of the car in NASCAR. On most NASCAR tracks where drivers make only left-hand turns, the inside and outside tires undergo different stresses. Formula 1 racing currently requires each tire to have four treads around it, but those rules might change in the future. They are required to have treads to decrease traction, which slows the cars down. Formula 1 cars are the only major racecar type to race in the rain. Of course, they change to more heavily treaded tires before resuming the race after it begins to rain.

Brain Fart

Most NASCAR races are similar to driving a taxi in New York City: hours of left-hand turns with an occasional fender-bender.

WHAT IS THE ADVANTAGE
OF NITROGEN IN TIRES?

Most racecar crew chiefs fill their tires with nitrogen, as do many truck drivers, bike racers, and the United States military. Using nitrogen in tires is even creeping into the everyday-driver market. Nitrogen is relatively inert (unreactive), especially when compared to oxygen. It's readily available and, therefore, relatively cheap; it makes up about 80 percent of the air around us. Nitrogen is dry out of a bottle, so no moisture gets inside the tire. Moisture in the tire vaporizes at high temperatures and expands, which would adversely affect the handling of the car. Nitrogen also migrates through the wall of the tire at a much slower rate than regular air, and best of all, it runs at a cooler temperature in a tire than regular air. All of these make nitrogen the choice of most racers.

If nitrogen is so great, how about filling your tires with helium? Your car/bike could just float down the road hardly touching the ground. You could decorate the tires with neat pictures, just like Mylar balloons. If helium works, hydrogen would be even better since it is the lightest gas. Of course, helium and hydrogen are flammable, so at a certain speed your tires would explode. Better stick to nitrogen.

HOW DOES DOWNFORCE HELP RACERS ON THE TRACK?

To understand downforce, we must first understand upforce (lift) on airplanes. Hold a paper money bill or strip of paper under your bottom lip and blow straight across the top of the paper. Why the bill rises is explained by the Bernoulli principle, which states that as the velocity of a fluid increases, the pressure decreases. Above the bill you have a lower pressure than under the bill, and lift is created. The airfoil of a wing creates lift for an airplane because of its shape. The air passes faster over the top of the wing so there's a lower pressure above the wing. The difference in pressure above and below the wing causes the wing to lift.

Racecars have inverted wings attached to their frame. By tilting these wings, the pit crews can help control the amount of downforce, which helps to increase friction with the road. Friction is desirable for traction and cornering. More friction means your tires won't spin and that you can drive faster through the corners.

Most single-car crashes occur at corners because drivers are going too fast. Driving too fast in a corner means the centripetal force is greater than the friction, so the car slides. The car will slide tangential to the circle and into the wall. At most racetracks you can see wall marks at each corner from crashes. However, most multicar accidents occur when one racer hits another racer. Men like racing, but they absolutely love a good crash, especially since the cars are so safe nowadays.

Racecar manufacturers do all that they can to keep their drivers safe, and that includes using the entire body of the car to help create downforce. NASCAR uses air dams to limit the amount of air passing under the body of the vehicle. The narrow area under the car creates high-velocity air under the car, which lowers the pressure so the higher-pressure air above the car pushes it down at high speeds. Formula 1 cars have bodies that are actually shaped like upside-down wings for the same reason. Airplanes actually take off at lower speeds than most high-end racecars!

Did You Know?

Drag racing got its start on the salt flats in California's Mojave Desert and gained popularity during World War II.

Dragsters have an interesting way of creating more downforce: They point the exhaust headers to the sky. The exhaust coming out pushes the car down into the track. More than half of their total downforce comes from this. It also creates a crowd-pleasing sight and a deafening noise. The exhaust gases will often light after they leave the headers for extra pyrotechnics. The dragsters also have a wing over the back wheels to generate more downforce.

WHY DO DRAGSTERS DO A BURNOUT?

Dragsters go through a burnout prior to entering the staging area. This cloud-inducing ritual is always a hit with guys. We get noise and a ton of smoke. However, in addition to amping up the crowd, the burnout serves a scientific purpose.

The dragster pulls into a puddle of water to wet the tires down. After pulling onto dry pavement, the brakes are locked and the throttle is opened up. The back wheels spin in place and create smoke. The tires also grow and expand as they heat up. Like most racecar tires, dragster car wheels are soft rubber. The expanded diameter helps the dragster cover more distance with each rotation of the tire. The burnout makes the tires stickier and cleans off any debris. It also wears out the tire quickly, but the top-level pros get them for free. The cars are equipped with a line lock, which allows the back brakes to be disengaged during the burnout, saving the back brake pads.

The tires are also only filled with 7 pounds per square inch (psi) of pressure. A normal car tire is usually filled to about 30 psi, and bike tires can be up to 100 psi. The low pressure causes the tire to look flat. The tires are actually called wrinklewalls because of this look. The flattened tire allows more of the tire to form a larger contact patch with the ground. A greater contact patch leads to greater traction. Cavemen may have started mankind on the way to racing for fun, but I doubt cavemen could envision the science in racing now.

Scientifically Speaking

When I raced a car last it was a time when sex was safe and racing was dangerous. Now it's the other way around.

—Hans Stuck

WHAT IS THE DIFFERENCE BETWEEN NITRO AND TOP FUEL?

Nitro is short for *nitromethane*, a popular fuel added into engines for increased horsepower. All hydrocarbons burn, but nitro (CH_3NO_2) has the added benefit of containing oxygen. That means it can burn using less outside oxygen. It delivers almost two and a half times the power of conventional gasoline. Nitro also vaporizes at a lower temperature, so the engine block is actually cooled by the nitro. Outside oxygen is usually the limiting factor in an engine's horsepower because it controls how much fuel is burned. Nitro helps solve that dilemma.

Nitro is used in street racers. It is also the largest component of top fuel that powers the long-rail dragsters. Top fuel is 85 percent nitromethane and 15 percent methanol. Top fuel burns fast and ferocious, just what speed demons want.

Brain Fart

If nitro is good for racing, wouldn't it be great for my gas grill? Just wait until everything else is on the table, kick in the nitro, and the steaks will be done. Of course, you also run the risk of your grill launching off your deck. Slow steaks or a grill in orbit? You can make that decision.

HOW DO SMART WALLS WORK?

As safety has risen to a new level, smart-wall technology has become standard on most racetracks. Racecar fatalities are now rare on the professional circuits due to this new technology and better head restraints. The head restraints redirect much of the initial energy away from the head and neck by keeping the movement of the head and neck to a minimum. New wall technology only adds to the safety factor.

New walls are smart. The outside concrete wall is now backed up by at least two inner layers. The innermost layer is composed of hollow steel beams that are strong but will crush in an extreme crash. The inner layer is made up of very high-density foam. In a head-on crash, the two inner layers act like a giant sponge to absorb the energy. The more time it takes to absorb the energy, the less force the driver feels. Safe-wall technology, although new to racing, has been used on many highways for over twenty years. Many exit ramps have bright yellow barriers filled with sand or water that are designed to crush if you hit them.

Most racecar crashes are glancing blows, which decreases the amount of force on the car and driver. Also, cars are designed to crumple only at certain points. Manufacturers just need to protect the cockpit area, called the driver's capsule. Many people equate racing with good old country boys. Well, they may be good old country boys, but they are backed by nerds with engineering degrees. Behind every good racecar driver is a calculator-carrying geek. Never pick on nerds and geeks. They may save your life one day!

Scientifically Speaking

I believe that a scientist looking at nonscientific problems is just as dumb as the next guy.

—Richard Feynman

WHAT IS A STOLEN VEHICLE RECOVERY SYSTEM?

If you drive a nice car, people will be jealous. Some may even try to steal it. A stolen vehicle recovery system works by hiding a GPS receiver (or computer chip) on your car. After the vehicle is stolen, the system can be activated to find the car's location. You will have to pay for the system's installation and a fee to monitor it. The receiver must be well hidden or the thieves will just disable it and sell it for a profit too. A cheaper stolen vehicle recovery system is buying a car no one would ever steal. A well-rusted 1991 Toyota Corolla may even be cheaper than the cost of a system. The added benefit of this method is you will get extra exercise. You're guaranteed to park this beauty out of the sight of your friends—and any first dates!

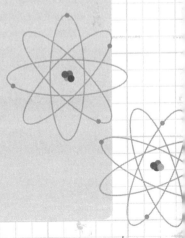

HOW DOES GPS WORK IN
YOUR CAR?

Guys are important to the future of the auto industry. After all, if not for the male refusal to ask for directions, GPS-aided navigational devices wouldn't be standard in all high-end automobiles. These marvels of technology help us on many levels. The fact that we don't have to stop the car to ask directions goes without saying, but we also get a sexy, computerized female voice telling us to turn right in three-tenths of a mile. Most guys hate backseat drivers, but we have no problems taking direction from that ever-so-sexy voice. We also, depending on the type of system, get a built-in television screen in the front seat. Guys would never watch television while driving, but it's nice to know we can watch it while waiting in line to pick up our daughter at school.

> ## Did You Know?
>
> President Ronald Reagan was responsible for opening up the commercial GPS market. After the downing of the Korean Air commercial plane in 1983 (for inadvertently entering the airspace of the former Soviet Union), Reagan issued a directive that the GPS signals would be freely available to the world when the system was ready.

And if you don't want to be ordered around by that sexy female voice, you have other options. Most units come with a choice of different voices. At least one manufacturer allows you to go online and choose celebrity voices. I can almost hear Bart Simpson's nasal voice saying "Turn right, dude." Or Yoda's contemplative voice saying "A tremor in the force I feel" as you make a wrong turn. SpongeBob may also be a good choice, but I wonder if all my drives would end up in the ocean. But how does your favorite voice know how to tell you what to do?

GPS stands for Global Positioning System and was developed for the military, but, luckily for guys, it was soon opened up to the general public. This system uses twenty-seven satellites orbiting the Earth that transmit data to receivers on the ground. Every square centimeter of the Earth's surface is visible to at least four satellites at any one time, and your GPS receiver calculates the distance to at least three (some units use four) of these satellites. From these different distances, the receiver uses a process called trilateration to combine these distances with the location of the satellites to determine the location of the receiver (your individual GPS unit). Think of the distance from one satellite as the radius of a circle. Another distance would be another circle. Those circles would only overlap at two points. A distance from a third satellite would give you the exact location of the receiver. Of course, in three-dimensional space the circles are actually spheres, but the concept is the same.

How a GPS Works

Your Location

Satellites

The location of your car can then be fed into the unit's database of maps, and the sexy voice will steer you to your destination. Many devices also preprogram locations of gas stations, restaurants, and cash machines into the database. A few databases even preprogram locations of known speed traps to help save you a ticket or two. These receivers are also useful for automotive security if your car gets stolen.

HOW DO ANTILOCK BRAKES (ABS) WORK?

If you are old (like me), you were taught to pump your brakes as you slowed. This is to prevent the wheels from locking up and your car from sliding uncontrollably. ABS electronically pumps your brakes, so none of the wheels ever slide. The best ABS systems use a sensor on each wheel to measure the rotational speed for that wheel. A sliding wheel does not rotate. As the sensor detects one wheel rapidly slowing (compared to the other wheels), a valve will shut off brake pressure to that wheel. This causes the wheel to keep rolling. The valve reopens when the wheel is spinning at the same rate as the others. The valve may open and close up to twenty times per second. The wheels keep spinning, and the car is easier to control as it comes to a stop.

In early ABS systems, you could actually feel the brake pedal pumping under your foot, but with newer systems this is no longer felt. You should never pump your brakes with ABS; it will just take you longer to stop.

The science of ABS was learned by most of us on a bicycle many years ago. If you locked up the wheels, you crashed into the side of Dad's hideous-looking car. By steering as you stopped, you could plow into a bush in the neighbors' yard. Crash landing into the bush was the bicycle equivalent of the air bag.

Scientifically Speaking

Isn't it interesting that the same people who laugh at science fiction listen to weather forecasts and economists?

—Kelvin Throop III

HOW CAN YOU DRIVE ON RUN-FLAT TIRES?

Run-flat tires, tires that will keep rolling even as they lose air (or nitrogen), are becoming more common. Newer technology can even handle blowouts with minimal loss of control. Run-flat tires use one or a combination of three separate methods. Self-sealing tires use a fluid that will seal any small punctures. The fluid reacts to the loss of air and plugs smaller holes. This fluid is actually sold separately in aerosol cans or is inside the tire originally. Self-supporting tires have very rigid sidewalls that support the entire car for short distances. Auxiliary supported systems contain a ring of rubber and/or polyurethane inside the traditional tire. Think of them as having a second tire waiting as backup within the outer tire. When air is lost, the car rides on the inner ring. These auxiliary supported systems are the surest handling form of run-flat tires. NASCAR already uses a similar system for its tires.

The best run-flat tires are on my lawn mower. I've never had a flat in thirty years of mowing lawns. You could just put big solid wheels on your Benz and roll down the road. Of course, your fillings would shake out of your teeth, but you'd never be stranded with a flat.

HOW DOES AN AIRBAG PUNCH YOU IN THE FACE?

For years, when I thought of the word *airbag*, my high school history teacher came to mind. Today airbags take on a new meaning. We are discussing the powder-exploding-in-your-face-save-your-life car air bags. Air bags save lives because of physics and chemistry. The physics behind an air bag is the same as trapping a soccer ball with your foot. All moving bodies contain momentum (the product of mass and velocity). To stop an object, you need to apply an impulse (the product of force and time). It takes the same impulse to stop whether you hit a tree or use the brakes. The key is time. If you increase the time, you decrease the force on the object. The airbag increases the time it takes your body to stop, so you feel less force. In the same way, moving your foot as you trap the ball decreases the force the soccer ball feels.

Air bags contain an accelerometer that measures rapid deceleration, like when you hit a tree. This accelerometer activates the airbag's chemical reaction to inflate the bag. The most common chemical used is sodium azide. When ignited, it releases harmless nitrogen gas into the nylon bag, very fast. The nylon deploys at speeds up to 220 miles per hour! Your body must be 10 inches away from the bag when it explodes to avoid serious damage. The bag increases the time your body takes to stop, and you feel less force. The bag also spreads out the force over a larger portion of your body, which helps spread the hurt out. The bag immediately starts to deflate the nitrogen through vents so you can get out of the car. Of course, you are left covered with talcum powder and maybe some fabric burns. This powder is used to lubricate the bag while the bag is folded up in your car. Think of it as being punched with a giant, padded, baby-powder-covered boxing glove.

Today many newer cars come with side airbags. Car scientists are experimenting with selective airbags, which deploy at different speeds for different crashes. These airbags will also deploy at different speeds based on where you are sitting on the seat. Remember, air bags should always be used with seat belts, and children should never be in the front seat. They are too small and could be hurt by the airbag.

You may be asking, "If airbags can help me survive, why can't they help my car survive?" Most men would love a car that had airbags mounted on the outside. When we start to hit something our car would explode into a balloon-covered ball of steel and nylon. We could bounce around like a carnival ride and our car would survive unhurt. James Bond once used a business suit like this to survive. NASA also used a similar setup to land a spacecraft on Mars. Why not use this same technology to save our cars?

WHAT DOES THE OCTANE NUMBER MEAN?

The octane rating on the gas you buy gives you a rating for spontaneous combustion. All gasoline vapor will eventually combust as it is compressed in the cylinder. Combustion before the spark plug ignites (knocking) is bad, since it will damage the engine and rob you of gas mileage.

All gasoline is made of long hydrocarbon chains. Octane (eight carbon atoms) and heptane (seven carbon atoms) are the most common ingredients in gasoline. An 87 octane number works very well in a normal low-compression engine like most of us have in our cars. The 87 means the gasoline is 87 percent octane and 13 percent heptane. You can also use any combination of hydrocarbons that reach the same octane result on a test engine. Higher-compression engines need a higher octane number to stop knocking and to deliver more horsepower. It is possible to even boost the octane number over 100 by adding other chemicals. The most common additive for years was a lead compound. But lead is bad for the environment so it is no longer added to automobile gas. It is still added to avgas, for airplanes, but scientists are currently working to find alternatives.

Scientifically Speaking

In these days, a man who says a thing cannot be done is quite apt to be interrupted by some idiot doing it.

—Elbert Green Hubbard

CAN YOU MAKE YOUR OWN GASOLINE?

With the fluctuating price of gasoline, you may wonder if it is possible to make your own. You can use a process called gasification that utilizes organic waste to make syngas (or synthetic gas, which you can then use to make gasoline), but it is easier to make ethanol that can power your car. Ethanol is just a simple form of alcohol that already makes up 5 to 15 percent of the gasoline we buy. So how do we make ethanol?

To make alcohol, you need a sugary/starchy food and some yeast. For the sugary/starchy stuff you can use corn, but corn is average in its starch content. Sugar cane is a much better choice. Yeast is living bacteria that devours the sugar or starch in your food. The yeast eats through the starch/sugar and excretes alcohol, water, and carbon dioxide in the fermentation process, leaving only alcohol and water. This is where your local moonshiner will come in handy. He has a still in the woods halfway up the hill behind his house. The still separates the alcohol from the water, so you are left with pure alcohol. Alcohol evaporates much easier than water. By heating the mixture, the alcohol is vaporized. The alcohol runs through a tube to another collecting device (we'll call it a jug). The water is left in the main kettle. The collecting jug will be full of pure alcohol. Pour it in your gas tank and away you go. Be sure to thank Billy Bob as you drive down the mountain. Note: To use pure ethanol in an auto engine, you'll need to purchase and install an ethanol conversion kit.

> **Did You Know?**
>
> Most of us think of moonshine as illegal corn liquor from the southern United States, but the word actually originated in England. Smugglers worked by moonlight as they brought in illegal liquor. What they were smuggling became known as moonshine. The word spread to America in the mid-nineteenth century and was used for liquor made to avoid taxes—or prohibitionists.

HOW DO YOU HOT-WIRE A CAR?

All men that go to acting school must learn how to hot-wire a car. Virtually all action movies end up with an otherwise law-abiding citizen hot-wiring a car to save the day, and this person also always ends up with a hot girl. I've got to get into acting school!

The concept of hot-wiring a car is fairly simple on older models. The starter, battery, and the ignition switch are all in a simple electrical circuit. The key allows you to close the switch to complete the circuit. You use the same process when you flip a light switch. To hot-wire a car, you simply cut the two wires going into the ignition. Strip back both wires a little, twist them together, and the circuit is complete. The engine roars to life. Of course, movies never show the guy getting shocked as he twists the wires together. Trust me; it would shock the pee out of you. It's never a good idea to twist together two wires in a live circuit, unless you are demented enough to like pain.

WHAT IS THE SECRET TO DIGITAL CHIP KEYS?

Newer cars are harder to hot-wire because they come with keys that contain a radio frequency transmitter. The key sends out a radio signal to your car that allows your key—and only your key—to start your car. Think of it like a second switch that's necessary to complete the circuit. The radio signal closes one switch and the key closes the other. Some models even scramble the radio code every time the key is used. This doesn't mean your car can't be hot-wired. Actually it could be hot-wired twice, once around both switches, but I don't think they teach the double hot-wire in acting school, yet.

A few super-high-end vehicles don't even need an ignition slot at all. The key stays in your pocket and you just press a button on the dash. The key transmits a radio signal that closes the circuit. Racecar drivers just press a button, which is too bad because it would be funny to see the Gran Prix of Monaco delayed because of a lost ignition key. You can even buy fingerprint readers that allow you to start your car without a key. Then the thief has to steal your finger to steal your car. Hopefully that's a deterrent.

> **Did You Know?**
>
> You can't get a replacement key for a Model T. Ignition keys weren't used on cars until the 1940s. Prior to that, the ignition was started by a crank or a pushbutton.

WHAT IS THE DIFFERENCE BETWEEN TORQUE AND HORSEPOWER?

No argument creates more passion among gearheads than torque versus horsepower. The fact is, they are related. Torque is a twisting force that doesn't require motion. It is measured out of the engine at the crankshaft by a machine called a dynamometer. Horsepower requires movement and is a measurement of the work and power an engine delivers. The unit horsepower was actually just a clever marketing gimmick to help James Watt sell his new steam engines in the late 1700s.

Car magazines list both torque and horsepower at certain revolutions per minute (rpm). At low rpms, torque is more important to get you moving. At higher rpms, horsepower is more important to keep the wheels spinning. Your transmission uses gears to maximize the power delivered to the road. The combination of torque, horsepower, and gearing is designed for specific needs. A farm tractor has incredible torque but low rpms. The tractor just crawls along, but it pulls easily. A high-performance car has incredible horsepower at high rpms but may have less torque than the tractor. For this reason, you never see a sports car pulling a plow.

In their love for speed, men will race tractors, but they race tractors against other tractors. The sight of a John Deere coming off the final corner in the next Indy 500 would be a funny sight. Guys will continue to debate torque and horsepower, but

Scientifically Speaking

All truths are easy to understand once they are discovered; the point is to discover them.

—Galileo

the truth is they are both important for different needs. When taking off from a red light, torque rules. On the Autobahn, horsepower rules. If you have car-nut friends, this argument can be comical. Just say "torque rules," then sit back and watch the fireworks. Be prepared; this argument may result in fisticuffs. Neither side will waver on their preheld belief.

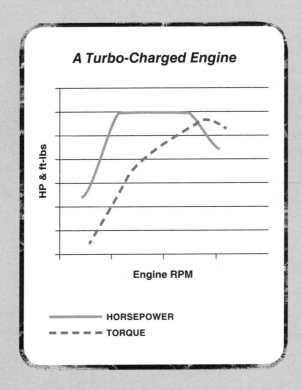

HOW DOES A CAR SELF-PARK?

For most people, the most feared part of a driver's test is parallel parking. Thankfully, new technology is taking the sweaty palms out of the equation. Using radar and a computer, some new cars are able to park themselves in any tight space. Radar waves locate the cars on both sides of the space, and the computer turns the wheels as you back into the space. You still control shifting gears, the gas, and the brake—at least for the time being.

Eventually cars will do all of the driving for us. We'll just sit back and let the car drive. If engineers can develop this, why not develop other man-friendly technology? A toilet seat that automatically lowers itself after guys do their business, automated diaper-changing tables for babies, and a self-mixing martini; all would be welcome in our world.

Brain Fart

Cars that parallel park themselves deprive pedestrians of the joy of watching people screw up.

THREE: GAME TIME

For many of us, sports represent a way of life. Even if we are only average players, guys revel in watching sports done well: watching Tiger Woods do things we never will, watching soccer stars dazzle us with their feet, watching human skyscrapers dunk basketballs like we dunk doughnuts. We secretly wish we could get paid millions to play a kids' game. We watch, we cheer, we go out and try to imitate them, yet most of us suck. But science is helping us suck less than we did before.

The science of sports has grown a hundredfold over the last fifty years. Computers are no longer the tools of just nerds. Engineers have turned their sights to round balls, bats, shoes, and all the things we use to make sports fun. Even things as mundane as clothes and bowling balls have been engineered for better results.

Sports-related items are a multibillion-dollar business. The high-tech science types spend tons of cash to develop ways to make our game better. It is funny that we buy into the mystique of fancier equipment. Most of us won't be pro players with fancier stuff, but we buy anyway. We gladly pay extra money for any piece of equipment that will help us beat our friends in a game. So lace up your sneakers as we examine the wonderful world of sports.

DO GRAPHITE SHAFTS HELP YOU HIT A GOLF BALL FARTHER?

Most of us who play golf waffle between a love of the sport and a hatred of it. We spend a Saturday alternately enjoying the game and cursing like a sailor, but most of us keep coming back to the course. Almost all golfers fall into three categories: pros, scratch golfers, and hacks. Pros make a living playing golf. Scratch golfers are good but don't make a living at the game. Hackers swing away and swing away. The ball seldom goes in the planned direction.

I think hackers get more enjoyment out of the game than the professionals. Before you put down this book, let me defend my point. You pay a certain amount for greens fees and a cart. Amateurs don't get a discount for using fewer strokes, so you get more bang for your buck. Hackers also get to enjoy all the parts of the course, including the backyards of a few people who live close by. Of course, a few amateurs want to be good so they invest many dollars into getting better.

We copy the pros and buy the best we can afford, but many times the clubs we buy—our largest financial investment in the game—aren't the best for us. A golf swing is all about transferring energy into the ball. Pros swing very fast and true and generate tons of energy from the speed of their swing. Most pros use a very stiff shaft so little energy is lost to flexing the shaft and vibrations after the ball is hit. Amateurs need a little more help.

When hitting the ball, speed is king because the primary energy is kinetic, and kinetic energy is related to the square of the speed. A faster clubhead delivers more energy to the ball, and the whip action a flexible shaft generates helps to create additional speed. As you get better and win a few dollars from your friends you can upgrade to stiffer shafts, but you might not get to see as much of the course.

Graphite, carbon fiber, and steel shafts can all be tailored to your game. Graphite is a good choice for many of us for two reasons: one, it is light so the club can be swung faster; and two, graphite is more flexible than steel so you can get good whip action. However, even though graphite can help you hit a ball further, the increased flexibility of the shaft is harder to control so you may sacrifice accuracy for distance. A personal note—all shafts will break when you hit a tree in anger.

Brain Fart

Hackers may actually enjoy the game of golf more than professionals since they get to hit more shots and see more of the course.

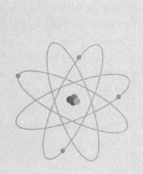

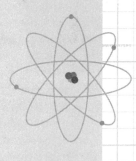

HOW DO LARGE GOLF CLUBHEADS HELP?

Large heads (for the golf club, you moron) result in longer drives. The key here is energy and momentum conservation. Titanium and exotic alloys help to make clubheads larger and lighter. A lighter clubhead can reach a higher speed, and a higher speed means more kinetic energy for the club. Additional energy for the club equals more energy for the ball. The ball goes farther.

A larger clubhead also gives you a larger sweet spot—the ideal place to strike the ball—on the clubface. The actual contact with the ball is all about momentum transfer. Momentum is the product of mass and velocity and is of utmost importance in collisions. A more massive clubhead gives you more momentum to deliver to the ball provided your swing velocity is high enough. Heavier clubs will slow your swing down, so you walk a tight rope between mass and velocity.

At least in golf, bigger is better. But too big is not worth the lost clubhead speed. You actually want to crush drives off the tee. Your buddies all watch as you tee it up. You can walk a little taller and stick your chest out further when you are long off the tee. And remember this rule of golf: If you don't reach the red tees, you must stick something else out.

CAN THREE-PIECE GOLF BALLS HELP YOUR GAME?

Balls are important in life and also in golf. Once you reach a certain level with your golf game, the ball can help take you to the next step. Ball scientists have spent years developing balls that will help your game and generate their company piles of cash. Golf actually started with players swinging at feather-filled sacks. We sure have come a long way.

The newest generation of balls contains three layers for increased performance. The thin, dimpled outer cover is soft, which allows for increased spin. The additional spin is especially important around the greens. The next layer is a hard mantle that helps transmit the club's energy into the core. The core is hard and designed for distance. Put it all together and you have a great ball for pros and scratch golfers.

For hackers, though, three-piece balls are probably not going to help. The increased spin will contribute to slicing and hooking and will cost you distance if your swing is slow. The soft cover will also tear if you mis-hit the ball. The ball will be left with a giant smile in the torn cover. These balls are expensive and will sink in the water. Most hackers could save a few dollars by playing floaters stolen from your favorite aquatic driving range. You also get an added benefit if you actually ever beat anybody with these balls. Can you imagine the embarrassment of being thrashed by a player using a ball with a red stripe? You are sure to be treated well at the nineteenth hole if you promise to keep the secret. The thrill of victory and free drinks.

Did You Know?

It's a myth that golf courses have eighteen holes because there are eighteen shots in a bottle of Scotch. The number of holes on any particular course originally varied from six holes to over twenty. Eighteen holes became the norm after golf clubs in England recognized St. Andrews, an eighteen-hole course, as the rule-making course in the late 1890s.

WHY DO THEY PUT DIMPLES ON A GOLF BALL?

Early golf balls were smooth. Golfers soon realized that a scuffed-up ball would actually fly farther. Many a golfer would take a little sandpaper to the ball to lower his score. Dimples were added and the rest is history.

There are two types of aerodynamic drag on any flying ball: friction and pressure drag due to air separation. Friction with the air is a given unless you play on the moon. Pressure drag due to air separation can be lessened if you can get the air to curve farther around the ball. Dimples do just this by grabbing boundary air and causing it to stay with the ball longer. The longer the boundary air stays curved around the ball, the less pressure drag there is. Less drag equals longer drives. Personal note from my twenty-year love-hate relationship with the game—dimpled golf balls still sink. I play red-striped balls and often finish a round with a Red Stripe.

Did You Know?

Thanks to supercomputers, you can now see how the air travels around a golf ball in flight. Go to the LiveScience website (*www.livescience.com*) and search for "dimple dynamics," then click on the video link entitled "The Secret of Golf Balls Revealed: Dimple Dynamics."

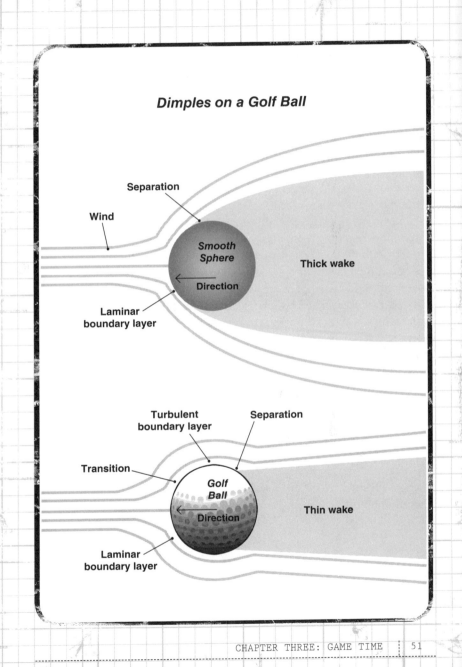

Dimples on a Golf Ball

WHY DO BASEBALLS CURVE?

Baseballs curve because of the spin of the ball. The Bernoulli effect states that in a fluid flow (such as the air around a baseball or airplane wing) an increase in the speed of the air results in a decrease in pressure, and conversely, a decrease in the speed of the air results in an increase in pressure. A right-hand pitcher spins a curve ball counterclockwise, and the spinning baseball will grab air and pull it along with the spin. Going with the spin will result in high-speed air (and low pressure) on the left side of the baseball. But some air will try to go on the other side against the spin, resulting in lower speed and higher pressure on the right side of the ball. This means the pressure on the right side of the ball is greater than on the left, which causes the ball to curve to the left.

The Magnus effect further describes spinning objects. According to the Magnus effect, because of the rotation of the ball, the air travelling around the ball redirects the wake behind the ball and helps to steer it. The air dragged along with the spin (and the stitches) causes lower pressure on one side of the ball. The redirection of the wake and the difference in air pressure cause the ball to rise in that direction. The stitches help because they assist in the pulling of air in a spinning ball. In the 1960s, professional baseball even lowered the height of the stitches to allow balls to curve less.

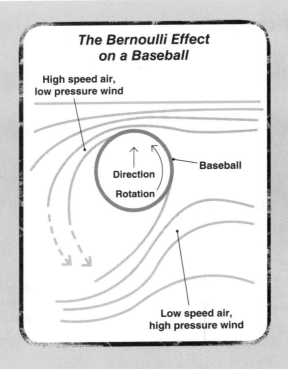

**The Bernoulli Effect
on a Baseball**

High speed air,
low pressure wind

↑ Direction

Rotation

Baseball

Low speed air,
high pressure wind

Pro baseball players can direct the rise in almost any direction to confuse the batters. A curve is thrown in an overhead direction, so the ball will curve downward. A perfectly flat curve could still be hit since the swing plane of the bat is flat. A slider is a hard-thrown ball that only curves slightly but is moving faster than a curve. A rising fastball is actually thrown with backspin. It doesn't rise at all; it just falls less than normal. But what if you threw a ball without any spin?

HOW DOES A KNUCKLEBALL WORK?

Knuckleballs float and dance on their way to the strike zone. When thrown correctly—which is very hard to do—they confuse hitters and leave them swinging at air. But how do they work?

Air doesn't slide over smooth surfaces very easily, but it slides over air swirls or turbulence very easily. Dimples on a golf ball allow the balls to trap air close to the ball in a boundary layer. This boundary layer essentially keeps small amounts of air glued to the ball. Knuckleballs combine the Bernoulli effect and boundary layers to make the ball dance. Knuckleballs spin very slowly, about one complete spin between the hand and home plate. The stitches create small swirls of air (turbulence), and these swirls allow high-speed air momentarily. But since the stitches move very slowly, this high-speed air (from the swirl) disappears a fraction of a second later. This means the areas of low pressure show up to curve the ball but quickly are gone, allowing the ball to change directions several times in its flight.

> **Did You Know?**
>
> Before 1872, baseballs were made of horsehide, rubber, and string, and ranged between a golf ball to a softball in size.

You can see knuckleballs in other sports like soccer, football, and volleyball. Any ball that doesn't spin will go on a wild ride. Almost every sports ball is not smooth, so you get the small swirls of air that create those wacky curves. Ping-pong balls don't knuckle even when they aren't spinning because the balls are completely smooth.

WHY ARE TENNIS BALLS FUZZY?

Fuzz on a tennis ball serves the same purpose as dimples on a golf ball. The fuzz creates small swirls of air very near the surface of the ball. These small swirls stick to the ball as it spins. The small swirls are called the boundary layer. Air will slide over these swirls of boundary air easily.

The balls will still curve to the Magnus and Bernoulli effects even with this boundary layer of air. Tennis balls are usually hit with plenty of topspin. A tennis player strikes the ball in an upward arc as the racquet goes from low to high. The racquet imparts topspin.

This topspin causes the ball to curve downward (thank you, Messrs. Bernoulli and Magnus). You can hit the ball hard and curve it back down into the court. Bernoulli and the boundary layer help you to be the best. And we owe it all to a little fuzz (and some science).

WHY DON'T THE YELLOW LINES IN FOOTBALL BROADCASTS SLICE THROUGH THE PLAYERS?

The visible first-down line in American football is one of the most amazing things added to sports telecasts in years. The yellow line clearly shows where your team needs to go and is now a staple of every broadcast.

The simple line actually takes a mountain of equipment and people to create—four people and a semitruck full of computers and monitors. A single company makes almost all of the yellow lines we see.

First a 3D model of the field is created by accurately taking measurements before the game. Many natural-grass fields are crowned (raised at the center for drainage), so that step is important. Next the cameras are mounted on sensors that relay all camera movements back to the semi. The raw feed then has the yellow line repainted over it at the appropriate spot sixty times a second to give us a solid line on the television screen.

Yellow lines are important because that color is the most visible color to the human eye and almost never used on football uniforms. The yellow line is only programmed to be drawn on the green shade of the turf. Therefore, when a player runs across the yellow line, his uniform colors stay true. So he can slice through the yellow line instead of the yellow line slicing through him.

Graphics have changed for sporting events a hundredfold in the last twenty years. Now we have fancy moving displays for racecars and tons of virtual graphics for football, baseball, and soccer. The yellow line is here to stay, and most of us are glad. It sure looks good on our 106-inch high-definition screens.

Scientifically Speaking

Men forget everything; women remember everything. That's why men need instant replays in sports. They've already forgotten what happened.

—Rita Rudner

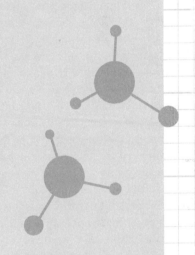

WHY ARE NEW TENNIS RACQUETS THE SIZE OF RHODE ISLAND?

Gone are the skinny wood racquets that dominated the game for years. Of course, they dominated the game because they were the only option. Starting in the 1970s, racquets began to grow to enormous proportions. The average tennis player wanted to get better, and science stepped in. Advances in materials and the growing popularity of the game were primarily responsible for this growth.

Larger racquets have larger sweet spots. But even the sweet spot has several parts. Close to the top of the sweet spot is a dead spot. This spot will transmit maximum vibrations to your arm but minimize the force on the ball. This is the perfect area for hitting a drop shot. Closer to the handle is the maximum bounce spot, giving the ball a maximum bounce for a minimum swing. This will give maximum bounce, but when you're swinging the racquet it is better to use more of the racquet. Between these two spots is the center of percussion. This area gives the least vibration to your arm and is the best overall spot to hit the ball since there is very little wasted energy.

The racquet is a long lever, and mechanical advantage is gained as the lever becomes longer. Think of it as opening a hinged door from the wrong side. It is very difficult to push open. The farther away from the hinge you push, the easier it is to open the door.

You can get different handle lengths for additional power, but a nice midsize racquet is good for most of us. The pros may benefit from smaller or longer racquets, but most of us won't.

HOW DO THEY CREATE NEAT GRASS DISPLAYS IN STADIUMS FOR SPORTING EVENTS?

Next time you watch a ball game, take a look at the amazing patterns created on the grass. The creativity has expanded beyond just stripes and lines. Grass now sports elaborate team logos and commemorative displays. The groundskeepers have elevated mowing to an art form. Just think Picasso on a lawn mower.

A heavy roller attached to the reels of the motor forms the patterns and shades. The roller can be lifted and lowered by a handle. Lowering the roller causes the grass to be bent in one direction. Rolling in the opposite direction will cause the grass to bend in the other direction. The sun will catch the grass at different angles and you have art.

Groundskeepers spend eighteen to twenty hours a day at the park. Creative mowing is just a fun way to break up the monotony of mowing the same grass everyday. It also gives the fans a neat backdrop. The downside is that it is only a matter of time before baseball teams start selling the space for advertising. Maybe in the future you'll be able to propose to your girlfriend using the Fenway Park outfield grass.

Scientifically Speaking

Why are things as they are and not otherwise?

—Johannes Kepler

HOW DOES THE CUE BALL COME BACK IN A BAR GAME OF POOL?

Ever since the first intrepid caveman turned his cave into the local pub, a single question has perplexed guys: How do they get the cue ball back in a coin-operated pool table? All of the other balls go into the hopper and won't be released until more coins go in the chutes, but the cue ball magically reappears after every scratch shot. And some of us in that cave (or pub) scratch quite a few times in a game. A purely anecdotal science hypothesis is that the number of scratches goes up as the ale goes down.

Early coin-op tables used heavier and larger cue balls. This method is still employed today for many tables. The cue ball is about ⅛-inch larger in diameter. As it rolls into the collecting chute, it strikes an overhead rail that deflects it into the cue ball opening. Simple and effective, but many good players don't like the larger ball. Newer tables use a cue ball with a magnet (or a metal core) to divert the cue ball. The ball is identical in size to the other balls but is usually heavier. Pool enthusiasts also claim the ball affects play. Magnetic balls also break easier. A few new machines use a laser to measure the amount of light reflected off the white cue ball. The white ball is kicked out before it reaches the collection trough. The white ball is exactly the same size and weight as the other balls, but chalk on the cue ball occasionally fools these sensors.

The average coin-op pool player sucks, but it is easier to blame the ball. You can also blame the lighting, alcohol, and local politicians. I blame my missed shots on plate tectonics. "Damn continental drift caused me to miss another shot."

HOW DO CLOTHES WICK AWAY SWEAT?

We sweat to keep our body from overheating during times of exertion. The layer of water on our skins cools us as it evaporates, but if it gets trapped in our clothes, we end up with a sweat-soaked shirt. In the good old days, cotton was the fabric of choice for working out. Cotton fibers are very good at wicking water away from your skin, but the sweat then gets absorbed into the cotton. The shirt will weigh five pounds after a few minutes of a particularly hard workout.

New fiber technology and design allows us to sweat without the buildup of water in our clothes. Engineered fabrics are created by virtually all of the fabric makers and are sold for performance clothing, bed sheets, and even nightgowns for menopausal women. Most of these engineered fabrics are constructed using similar design features.

First, the individual fibers don't absorb sweat the way cotton does. Second, the fibers are woven in such away to allow wicking channels to draw moisture away from the skin. And third, the exterior of the fabric is coated with a chemical that attracts water. The sweat is pulled up away from the body, and the airflow through the fabric allows the sweat to evaporate faster.

With sports clothing being a multibillion-dollar business, we are guaranteed to see further advances every year. These clothes help make sports better for us amateurs who begrudgingly pay too much for engineered clothing that helps improve our game. Engineered fabrics are even starting to show up in dress clothing. In the future, an engineered suit may help you sweat your way through your next job interview.

HOW DOES EYE BLACK HELP ATHLETES?

Eye black cuts down on the glare coming off your cheek. We wear dark clothes in the winter because black absorbs almost all the light that hits it. Ballplayers wear eye black for the same reason. Studies have shown that the black spots cut down on the amount of light that enters the periphery of an athlete's eye. This increases your contrast sensitivity, which helps when you are trying to track a high-speed ball. Curiously, studies seem to show that smudging greasy eye black under the eye works better than using a black bandage.

> **Did You Know?**
>
> Eye black works better for women and for people with dark eyes.

Originally ballplayers used burnt cork or shoe polish to smudge their face. Newer grease concoctions use paraffin and charcoal powder to absorb the light. Even more popular today are the small patches made of a patented dull black fabric. Of course, many athletes are turning these patches into advertising for friends, zip codes, spiritual messages, and so on. Which begs the question: Do you still get a big advantage from the black patch if you write on it with a white marker? I think not. But you might earn some points with your friends.

HOW DOES A SWIMSUIT HELP YOU SWIM FASTER?

Engineered fabrics don't just help you shed sweat; they can help in other ways. What about a swimsuit that repels water? High-tech swimsuits for professionals do that and more.

The suits are created with a fabric that repels water. By repelling water, the suit won't absorb any, so it stays as light as possible. The fabric is similar to the fabric used in high-tech rain gear. The holes in the fabric are too small for water molecules to penetrate. They are also coated in a chemical, similar to Teflon, which makes the water slide off. The swimsuits are also made with welded seams, which are thinner than a traditional sewed seam. The flatter seam allows less drag.

The suits also compress the entire body just like your grandmother's girdle. Compressing the swimmer's body means less drag. Racers spend up to fifteen minutes putting the suit on and use two helpers to do this. One holds and compresses while the other zips up. Your grandmother managed to do this by herself, so she must be more talented. I'd actually like to see my grandmother in lane eight at the next world championships in her white girdle.

The suits cover swimmers from their shoulders to their ankles and have much less drag than shaved skin. They will eventually cover the arms and head as companies do more research. Currently swimmers still wear a cap and keep their arms bare, but that will change as science helps us swim faster. It still takes training and ability to be the best, but science is helping lower the world-record times.

Brain Fart

We're not talking about the male Brazilian banana hammock here; we're talking about the full-length body suits that world-class swimmers wear.

HOW DO ALUMINUM BATS HELP LITTLE LEAGUERS HIT THE BALL FARTHER?

Gone is the crack of the wooden bat (except at the pro level). It has been replaced by an aluminum ping. Aluminum and high-tech composite bats have larger sweet spots and allow batters to hit the ball farther. But how?

One, they are hollow, which means that they're lighter and can be swung at a higher speed. Higher speed means more bat energy. Smaller kids can also use longer and wider bats because of the decreased weights. This makes it easier to hit the ball.

Two, these bats have larger sweet spots. The sweet spot is the point on a bat where the vibration into your arms is minimized and maximum energy is transferred to the ball. Wooden bats have a small sweet spot because wood bends relatively easy. Hard to imagine, but a wood bat actually flexes like a jump rope as you hit the ball. If you hit the ball off this sweet spot, your arms will feel a great deal of vibration and your hands sting. Aluminum bats are stiffer, so they don't flex as much. Because of this, aluminum bats have a larger sweet spot.

Three, they are helped by the trampoline effect. The ball and bat both flatten out as the ball hits the bat. The ball springing back to its round shape helps it jump off of the bat at a faster speed. Aluminum bats actually help this by causing the ball to deform more, giving it a faster rebound time.

Composite bats have actually taken many of these traits to a new level and must now be certified for safety reasons. Bats that transfer too much energy back to the ball have been outlawed by the major youth baseball organizations. At younger levels, they also use softer balls to make the game safer.

Even the major league game is wrestling with safer bats. A few years ago, many players started to shift from bats made of ash to bats made of kiln-dried maple. The maple bats are lighter and stronger, which means in the right hands the ball could travel farther. But maple bats shatter and send flying shards around the infield and into the stands.

I think to make the game safer major-league players should go to the gigantic green plastic bats that many of us first learned with. Or perhaps we should play the game with superballs or dress every player in catcher's gear.

Did You Know?

According to the rules, bats for major league baseball must be forty-two inches long or less. The longest baseball bat is 120 feet long, weighs 68,000 pounds, and is located at the Louisville Slugger Museum in Kentucky.

HOW CAN A BOWLING BALL HELP YOU STRIKE OUT THE SIDE?

Even a simple game like bowling has been improved by science. Most bowling balls today have a resin cover instead of the traditional urethane cover, which allows the average bowler to throw a few more strikes. And don't we bowl just for the strikes? Watching all the pins lie down flat is a pleasure.

Resin-covered balls essentially slide down the first half of the alley. The first half of the alley is oiled every day to help save the lane. On the oil, the resin balls have a lower coefficient of friction. On the dry second half of the lane, the resin balls have a higher coefficient of friction. This causes the ball to start turning more at a later point and impact the pins from a sharper angle. The impact angle of the ball helps deliver momentum. A greater angle in the pocket means the pins will move sideways—the key to a strike. Essentially, resin balls allow average bowlers to curve the ball at the end more, which results in more strikes. And more strikes equals more bragging rights.

> ### Did You Know?
> Frozen turkey bowling is a popular fundraising event in the winter months in many communities. Roll a frozen turkey toward ten pins for the chance to win a turkey. Hopefully it's a different turkey than the one you just bowled a strike with.

The interior of balls also have different-shaped cores, which help with the spin dynamics. Cores used to be spherical, but many are now dumbbell, elliptical, or light-bulb shaped. The cores can be matched with your strength to make a ball spin more. For years, bowlers created spin with strength and arm speed. Now science has leveled the playing field—the bowling alley. Just like in golf, visit the local pro shop to get matched up with the correct stuff. And better stuff can make you play the game better.

FOUR: BURPS, FARTS, AND THE SCIENCE OF SEX

The human body, brain, and all the appendages might be the most complex system ever made. The ability to think, reason, and react in a fraction of a second is absolutely amazing. It is estimated that a computer would need a thousand times the calculating power of a super-computer to even do half of what we do every day. So that means at two thousand times the calculating power, they could replace us. With the way computers improve by leaps and bounds, we may be obsolete in a few years.

Guys spend many hours admiring the human body—our own and others. We may not know all of the inner workings, but we enjoy the sights, sounds, and smells that are created by this marvelous machine. The human body and the things that make us unique will never be completely replaced by machines. Could you imagine some nerd-boy sitting in a lab trying to get his computer to fart? Actually I can, and he would be laughing the entire time.

Women do not understand our fascination with body creations, and they never will. That is one of the great things that make us different. Of course, guys don't understand the need for pedicures, either. So I guess we are even. Anyway, let's examine all the things that guys need to know about the human body. We need a starting point, and it may as well be the colon. The colon is a guy's best friend. We all laugh, joke, and share the wealth of all things related to this great body part. So put your gas mask on as we examine the wonderful world of the male body.

HOW ARE FARTS CREATED?

Farts cause guys to laugh. We may be a crude lot, but we do know funny. Even the word itself makes me laugh. However, there are many other ways to say the word *fart*. *Passing gas* makes the most sense. *Poot* and *toot* are other common euphemisms. *Flatulence* is the clinical term used by physicians for excess gas in the intestines. So maybe farting should be called flatulating. *Cutting the cheese* makes no sense to me. I have eaten stinky cheese but nothing that resembles a good poot. *Poot* is the term I am teaching my daughter, since she will invariably say the word at the wrong time.

Farts are created by gas in the intestines. This gas comes from a variety of sources. We swallow gas as we are eating or drinking. Carbonated drinks help this process along. Gas also seeps through the intestine wall into the food we ate. Gases are also created as we digest food and by bacteria that live in our intestine. Next time you complain about your neighborhood, just think, you could be living in an intestine. Makes your neighborhood seem a little nicer, doesn't it?

Farting ability differs from person to person. A certain relative of mine (who shall remain nameless) is a legend for his butt gas prowess. He can fart on cue at all times of the day and night. He would be world class at fart poker. For the uninformed, fart poker is a game we played in college. When one person farted, the rest of the room had a minute to ante up and pay one dollar to the farter, unless they could see the fart and raise the bet by farting themselves. Then they get the dollar by seeing the fart, unless they were raised again. The problem with being a great farter is that you can't turn off the gas pump. They pop out at the most inconvenient times. Of course, if you are adept at controlling the sounds, you can sneak the blame onto unsuspecting friends.

WHY DO FARTS MAKE A SOUND?

The ability to control the sounds emanating from your anus is a skill, a skill that will be admired by all of your guy friends. Farts make sounds by a process similar to the reed in the mouthpiece of an oboe. The vibration of the opening creates the sound. *Opening* is a politically correct term for butt hole.

The sound can take many different forms. Your sphincter muscles control the tightness of your anus. The tightness allows you some control over pitch. A tighter opening equals higher pitched poots. High-velocity gas can also lead to a higher pitch. The sounds range from SBDs (silent but deadly) to rafter-shaking bass notes. Timbre (quality) of the sound is related to the quality of gas, the size of your butt cheeks, and the clothes you have on. All three go together to determine tonal quality.

If you are adept at controlling the sounds, you can sneak the blame onto unsuspecting friends. This is a truly admired guy skill. I taught with a guy who was very adept at sneaking a fart off in class. The class would invariably blame someone else, never the offending teacher. He really was a truly fabulous teacher—great at leading class discussions with the ability to add a dose of levity when needed.

Brain Fart

The speed of a fart leaving the sphincter can change the timbre and pitch of the sound.

WHY DO FARTS SMELL?

The old joke is that farts smell so deaf people can enjoy them too, but it goes deeper than that. The smells come mostly from aromatic sulfur compounds in the gas. Farts contain carbon dioxide, oxygen, nitrogen, hydrogen, methane, and other trace gases, but the smell producer is primarily hydrogen sulfide.

Some foods create more gas than others. Broccoli, cauliflower, meat, eggs, milk, and beans are all good for farting. Beans are the all-time king of fart foods, but bean farts aren't always the most aromatic. Beans contain sugars that are broken down in the intestines and gas is created. Vegetables usually cause you to poot more, but they aren't as potent. Matter of fact, much of the roughage of plant material will be broken down in the intestines and create gas. They just aren't as smelly as protein-based farts.

> ## Brain Fart
>
> The word *fart* comes from the Old English *feortan* (meaning "to break wind").

Cow's milk is the king fart food for many people. Cow milk contains lactose, not present in mother's milk. Lactose is broken down by the enzyme lactase, and many people are actually lactose intolerant. They do not produce enough lactase, and a few don't produce any at all. All of the lactose must be broken down in the colon, and this breakdown produces gas . . . a lot of gas. Be careful! *Never* offer to take these people out for ice cream unless you are eating and leaving.

HOW DO YOU LIGHT
A FART?

Of course, you can light a fart. Many farts contain methane and hydrogen, both of which are flammable. The question is why you would want to. Open flame dangerously close to your private parts is just not smart. Usually fart-lighting episodes occur among people who have had a little liquid courage, but not always. Some guys purposely set out to light the gas just to see if it is possible. Never in recorded history has there been a documented case of a woman attempting this stunt.

This is an extremely dangerous stunt and should only be tried by trained professionals. You need the ideal setting and safety clothing. We are talking state-of-the-art flameproof suits like racecar drivers wear. You could even write letters to all of the *Fortune* 500 companies requesting sponsorship.

A doctor's exam table complete with stirrups is the ideal place for fart lighting; even better would be a birthing chair. A cauliflower-cheese-broccoli omelet may help the process along, so stop at your favorite diner on the way to the doctor's office. Get comfortable on the table with your feet up. Hold a lighter under your leg directly in front of your anus. Yelling "Freebird" as the lighter burns will help the process. Let 'er rip and watch the flareup.

Take note of the color to indicate different trace gases. Methane burns blue. Sulfur and sodium will give yellow hints to the flame. Copper traces will burn green. Potassium will give purplish tints to the flaming gas.

Seriously, burning farts is dangerous and should only be tried by professionals. A better way to see this is to go to one of the video-sharing websites and type in "burning farts." You get to see others risk their butt hairs for your enjoyment.

I have a new name for burning flatulence—"afterburners," since flaming flatulence looks like an afterburner from a jet engine. In theory afterburners could be the solution to the energy crisis. Afterburners are a perfect way to help power a car. Just attach a funnel from the driver's seat to the fuel injectors. It's a guy-powered hybrid automobile. Just like a hybrid, the oil-based gasoline could assist when your bean-based gas just isn't enough. Flaming flatulence adds a whole new meaning to the term *biofuel*.

Another benefit is that methane is a greenhouse gas. Lighting farts is going to get rid of some of the methane, which further helps the planet. Planting more beans and broccoli to fuel this afterburner–hybrid car phenomenon is also a good thing. The additional plants will suck up more carbon dioxide, which helps to eliminate some of that greenhouse gas. Maybe lighting farts should no longer be a college stunt but a way to save the planet. Flame on.

Brain Fart

Fart lighting should only be tried by professionals. Wonder where you get that degree?

WHAT IS A SNART?

A snart is a combination of sneeze and fart. These usually happen on a particularly gassy day when you sneeze. The muscles contractions of your sneeze forces gas out the other end at the exact same instant. Although momentarily painful, there are no reported deaths ever from a snart.

While an occasional fart makes us laugh, snarts never do. Both are natural processes that are better left separate. Funny thing, there is very little research that I can find on snarts. If you know any good PhD candidates looking for a thesis, snarts need to be delved into. We have already discussed farts, so let's take a look at sneezes.

You feel it coming, the tingling. It's coming and you can't stop it. You hold up a hand to your friends and take a step back. You rush to cover your nose with the other hand. Your nose explodes in a violent hailstorm of mucus and sound. Your friends bless you because of the mistaken notion you were momentarily close to death. You shake your head in dismay, and if you are like me, prepare for another. I have never single-sneezed in my life.

The nose is a mini air purifier. So when viruses, bacteria, dust, smoke, or other allergens enter your nose, the sneeze helps to clear the air. The sensitive linings of your nose send a signal to your brain to get rid of the offending material. The signal goes from the brain and then to the muscles, and all of this takes time. We feel the tingle and we know it is coming.

The muscles of the lungs contract, the mouth is sealed off, the vocal cords close, and your body spasms. That spasm causes virtually every muscle in your body to contract to get rid of the offensive material. Sneezing is an incredible abdominal workout.

The wonderful sound of a sneeze is brought out by the rapid rush of air as it leaves and your mouth opening to allow more air in. The sounds run the gamut from golf clap to jackhammer strength. Most of us have at least one friend whose sneezes are comical. I have a friend who goes from manly man to Celine Dion in the flash of a sneeze. I now realize that I am helping him if I can make him sneeze. He gets pure air and great abs. I am putting on cheap cologne next time I see him. I just have to make sure he isn't gassy before we hang out. Snarts aren't supposed to be dangerous, but who wants to take that chance?

HOW DOES ERECTILE DYSFUNCTION WORK (OR NOT WORK)?

Erectile dysfunction. The two words together just make guys laugh . . . well, at least some guys. And I have never heard a woman laugh at those words, only guys. I am not saying women don't laugh, I've just never heard them.

To understand erectile dysfunction (ED), we first have to understand erectile function (EF). An erection is as simple as blowing up a balloon. Normally the arteries going into ~~Mr. Happy, Big Willie, King Kong~~ your penis are somewhat constricted and the veins are wide open. Virtually no blood accumulates. When you are aroused, the cycle reverses. Like a balloon fills with air that can't escape, your penis fills with blood that can't escape.

The corpora cavernosa (penis) was empty before, but it is now full of blood as you stand at attention. Just look at the term *corpora cavernosa*. In Latin, this translates to "cave-like body." Filling this cave with blood leaves less blood for the brain, so your decision-making skills could be rendered momentarily suspect. The mechanics of increasing and decreasing blood pressure in the penis is at the heart of dys-function problems. Relaxing the arteries going into the penis is the goal of most ED drugs.

Until the early eighties, the problem was thought to be in the brain. Dr. Giles Brindley changed all that by injecting his penis with phentolamine, giving him an almost instant erec-tion. He dropped his trousers to show the world—ok, not the world, just a bunch of pee-pee doctors (urologists)—what he had figured out. He used the drug to relax the arteries going into his penis and BOING. The race was on for researchers to find a magic pill that could do the same thing. It turned out to be a blue pill—the best-known drug in the world—although other meds work as well.

Phentolamine doesn't give you a choice, but ED meds do. Also, the thought of injecting your penis with a needle isn't an option most men would ever go for. So how does the pill know to work only when you are worked up? The key is in the chemistry of muscle relaxations. Your brain controls the release of commands to make this happen. When a signal is sent to any muscle to relax the arteries, a chemical reaction starts. The chemical reaction causes an enzyme (cGMP) to react, which allows the muscle to relax. Another enzyme (PDE) works to destroy the cGMP. The PDE produced in the penis is different than other forms of PDE in your body, and the little blue pill can, thankfully, stop the penis PDE for a short time while you stand proud.

The blue pill has potential side effects of blurred vision and headaches. That is because penis PDE and head PDE are similar, so some people have head problems when they take the blue pill. Another, worse, side effect is a heart attack, so read and follow the directions. Other drugs are on the market and use slightly differ-ent chemicals to achieve the same result, but they also have some side effects. Moral of this story: Don't buy pills because of an e-mail. Talk to your doctor to find the cause of the issue.

Trust me, when erectile dysfunction comes to your house, you won't laugh. My motto has always been better living through chemistry. We may laugh about them until we need them, but disposable diapers and ED meds will both help us later in life.

Brain Fart

Erectile dysfunc-tion: If you take a pill to help get a "little lead in your pencil," you don't laugh when you hear those words.

CAN DEAD GUYS GET ERECTIONS?

While some live people struggle to get a woody, corpses can sometimes get them with ease. A death erection is also known as angel lust. It has been observed in cases of hangings and strangulations. Coroners have also discovered it in corpses that die face down.

The erection on a face-down corpse is easy to explain: gravity. The penis is just spongy tissue that fills with blood due to gravity if you die face down. Blood will always pool at the lowest point once the heart stops pumping.

The strangulation erection is thought to be caused by pressure on the spinal cord or cerebellum. Spinal cord injuries very often lead to a drop in blood pressure due to a loss of muscle tone in the blood vessels. This drop in pressure causes blood to pool in the extremities. For most guys, that extremity is the penis. This phenomenon was noticed at public hangings as many victims would develop erections as they swung from the noose.

HOW DO DISPOSABLE DIAPERS WORK?

I am not sure who invented them, but after you have a baby you will worship them. After all, the average diaper will soak up more than a liter of water. Guys are quick to change the diaper when there is poo in it but are a little slower for wee-wee. (Memo to my beautiful wife—except for me, I change it hourly.) The reason? Better technology. Babies don't get wet anymore. We were in the hospital for a full day and worried that our star hadn't gone. Turns out she had, there just wasn't any wetness. You actually have to pinch the outside of a diaper to see if it is full. Better living through chemistry.

Today's disposable diapers contain an inner layer of wicking material. This is similar to high-tech athletic gear that wicks the moisture away from your body. The wee-wee is wicked away from the privates and soaked into the diaper. The diaper contains sodium polyacrylate, a chemical that can absorb 200 to 300 times its own weight in water. Sodium polyacrylate is a polymer that is composed of identical shapes and sizes. When water is added to the chemical it is drawn toward the center of these identical chains and trapped. Urine will actually fill a diaper up faster than pure water because urine contains salt, which causes the sodium saturation to be reached quicker. This stops the trapping of the water. Trust me, diapers will leak after they become saturated.

This cool chemical is the same one used in florist gel, super-grow toys, and astronaut diapers. That answers the old joke: How do astronauts go to bathroom in space? Depends.

> **Did You Know?**
>
> The disposable diaper was invented by a woman, Marion Donovan. But Dow Chemical Company improved it by adding the absorbent chemical, sodium polyacrylate.

WHY DO BURPS HAPPEN?

Much like farts, burps come from extra gas that we swallow. As we eat, we not only swallow food and drink but also air and other gases. The pressure in our stomachs builds up due to this extra gas, and the body burps to relieve pressure.

The valve at the top of the stomach opens like a safety valve to let some gas go. A particularly good burp will even leave a taste in your mouth as it leaves. It may be socially unacceptable in many circles, but it beats popping like a balloon. It is okay to burp if you are under three or over eighty-three years of age. When a baby burps, people in the room cheer. When a senior citizen burps everybody laughs.

Don't we deserve applause or laughter when we let a good one rip? Many of us can do the alphabet or sing the "Star Spangled Banner" in one single belch. We've spent years developing this skill and should be rewarded with adulation.

Did You Know?

Scientists committed to stopping global warming are currently looking for ways to decrease the amount of methane that cows burp into the atmosphere by giving them foods that create less gas.

IS HOLDING A SNEEZE DANGEROUS?

I asked four doctors and none had ever signed a death certificate with sneezing listed as a cause of death. So I can confidently say that holding a sneeze won't kill you. Sneezes are funny. Watch people when they sneeze and you are guaranteed to chuckle.

Even though it won't kill you, holding a sneeze could cause you to blow your eardrums out. The extreme pressure inside your head needs to be vented somewhere. It is an urban legend that your eyes would pop out, unless it was a volcanic sneeze.

You can stop a sneeze with the finger-to-the-upper-lip trick. Here are other ways to stop sneezes. Don't breathe! Simple and effective, but it can lead to death if done long enough. You can also press your tongue tightly to the roof of your mouth, play with your ear lobe, or loudly say the word *watermelon* three times. This works and gives anyone within earshot a good laugh. Force your eyelids to stay open. Your body will never let your eyeballs pop out.

Did You Know?

It is impossible to sneeze with your eyes open.

Of course, these methods only work with sneezes that you feel coming on. The quick, immediate sneeze is going to happen occasionally. I think you should just let all sneezes go. You will feel better and your friends will get something to laugh about. After all, laughter is the best medicine.

WHY DO PEOPLE SNEEZE WHEN THEY WALK INTO BRIGHT SUNLIGHT?

Since day one I have always sneezed the second I walk into bright sunlight. On a summer day, I walk outside and immediately blow mucus and snot all over the place. I always sneeze three times; others affected sneeze more or less. I suffer from something doctors call the photic sneeze reflex. It's also called the ACHOO syndrome, a much better name in my opinion. *ACHOO* stands for autosomal dominant compelling helio-ophthalmic outburst. Anyway, numbers vary by study, but approximately 18–40 percent of all people suffer from this condition. It is genetic, and you have a 50 percent chance of passing it on to your kid.

The sneezing issue is probably caused by the link between the optic nerve and the sneeze nerve. The sneeze nerve is a nontechnical term for the trigeminal nerve. Some people appear to have a crosslink between these nerves since they run in close proximity in the head. The rapid constriction of your pupils causes the optic nerve to go into overload, and somehow that causes the sneeze nerve to react.

> **Did You Know?**
>
> The term *ACHOO* is called a backronym. Backronyms are created backwards from the original terms. You just hunt around until you find cute words that lead to the desired acronym.

Some researchers think the sneeze reflex is linked through the nose directly by tears. The eye constricts and releases a tiny amount of tears into the nose. The tears irritate the nose and you sneeze. Personally, I'm not so sure it could happen that fast. I sneeze too quick for tears to be the cause. Besides, I don't sneeze during sappy chick flicks. I am a sensitive guy and I cry sometimes. Now leave me alone.

WHY DO MEN THINK ABOUT SEX ALL THE TIME?

Guys think about sex all the time because our urge to procreate is deeply rooted in our inner beings. It isn't our fault; its biology. Almost all animals have an overwhelming need to continue their species. Men are no different, and it's a comforting thing to blame our desires on something other than our brain. The desires are a direct result of nature's designs. Sperm is good for seventy-two hours, but the egg is only good for twenty-four, so we have to work all the time to continue the species. Even if you don't want kids, the need is contained in your DNA. So we still think about it.

I heard a long time ago that on average men think about sex every seven seconds. I don't believe that number, it seems too short. Of course, once you factor in all the teen boys in this country, it is probably longer for the rest of us. In my older age I have been known to go at least three minutes without thinking of sex. The Kinsey Reports actually said that only 54 percent of men thought about sex even once a day. They call that report the bible of sex research, but it came out in 1948! In 1948 we had very limited television, no bikinis, and no Internet porn. But maybe they were right. So if they're right and the seven seconds is also right, some guys are doing way more than their fair share!

> **Did You Know?**
> Humans and dolphins are the only animals that have sex for enjoyment.

WHAT IS THE PROSTATE PROBE?

The word *digital* conjures up thoughts of high-end audio and video equipment, but it has other, not so pleasant, meanings. And one of those different meanings is found in the doctor's office. When men reach a certain age, all physicals contain a digital rectal exam. Digital in this case means digit, as in finger. And rectal means, well, rectal. The prostate probe is a necessary evil that is really beneficial.

The doctor takes a gloved, lubricated finger and probes into your nether regions to check your prostate gland—a walnut-shaped organ that helps in ejaculation—for abnormalities. Catching these abnormalities early is beneficial because treatment done early is almost always successful. The test only takes a minute. You drop your pants and your doctor begins to probe. Just be careful. If the lights dim and the speakers start playing Marvin Gaye music, you know it's time to get out of there.

Scientifically Speaking

But in science the credit goes to the man who convinces the world, not to the man to whom the idea first occurred.

—Francis Darwin

WHY DOES HAIR GROW OUT OF OUR NOSE AND EARS?

Hair has been in those places all along. Nose hair serves as a filter for the air we breathe in. In a dust storm, we could easily close our mouths, but closing your nostrils is downright hard. So nature built in a little air filter. Ear hair also is designed to keep junk out of the ear canal. Most men notice that their head holes seem to become more full of hair as they age. We pluck, trim, cut, tweeze, and it just keeps growing back. You can have permanent hair removal done, but you're a guy so you won't. The amount of medical research into ear and nose hair is surprisingly scant, so I'll just give you my two theories.

First theory: The adult body has a certain amount of hair follicles for its entire life. As you age, follicles migrate. Some inner working of the body causes you to lose hair on the top of your head, and gravity causes it to migrate south. As it migrates south, it vacations in warm, moist places like the nose and the ears. This is similar to going to the beach when you were younger—a wet, warm place to hang out. So the nose and ears are like going to the French Riviera for hair follicles. Only the lucky follicles get to hang out at the beach, until they get attacked by a giant weed eater called a nose hair trimmer. The problem with this theory is that the hair follicles also migrate to your back, which would be more like the desert. Of course, in the United States, many old people move to Arizona, Las Vegas, and Palm Springs. So maybe the hair follicle migration theory makes sense.

Brain Fart

Hair grows in your nose, like plants grow in a rainforest. They both shoot up fast in those wet, warm environments.

Second theory: Warm, moist areas grow hair better. The nose and the ear are both, so they make fertile areas for growing hair. You can think of the ear and nose as warm, wet garden plots. Most plants grow best in warm, moist areas, so this makes sense. You can think of back hair as cacti and aloe plants. The warm-moist theory postulates hair will always grow in the nose and ears, and it just becomes noticeable as we age. It was always present, but our thick head of high school hair distracted people away from focusing on it. Each day our head gets baked in the sun and dries out a little. The warm, moist hair just keeps growing along. As we lose hair on our scalp, the hair growing from the nose and ears becomes noticeable. By midlife it is far more noticeable because of less competition.

The actual reason of shifting hormone levels isn't nearly as much fun as making up theories. Any professional research scientist reading this might want to consider writing a grant to study this offensive hair. You can start with my two theories. Until then, I'll be tweezing away on the forest of hair growing from each nostril.

HOW DOES SMILING CONSERVE ENERGY?

We have all heard the adage about it taking fewer muscles to smile than frown. Muscles use energy. Just work out and you will agree with this fact. Adenosine triphosphate (ATP) is the primary energy-transfer molecule in your muscles, and your muscles can store four to six seconds worth of ATP to contract fibers. Using more muscles requires your body to work to create more ATP. If you use fewer muscles, you will use less ATP and save energy.

Although physiologists disagree on the exact number of muscles required for smiling and frowning, most agree that smiling takes fewer muscles. Smiling takes anywhere from four to fifty muscles, and frowning takes between thirty-three and one hundred. One expert disputes the finding, but most agree that smiling is easier. So smile and save energy. Of course, it only takes five muscles to express your feelings with a one-fingered salute.

Scientifically Speaking

If a man smiles all the time, he is probably selling something that doesn't work.

—George Carlin

WHY DO WE SLEEP?

Sleep researchers agree that sleeping is way more active than was once thought. When your body sleeps, your brain actually goes to work. While you sleep, growth hormone is excreted, which is needed to build up your body. This is the number-one reason babies and infants need more sleep. Growth hormone helps your body rebuild your muscles while you sleep, and during this rest time your body also restores used-up energy supplies. You can think of sleep as a tune-up for your body.

REM (rapid eye movement) sleep is extremely active. During this period of sleep, your brain is almost as active as it is when you are awake. This is when the brain does most of the dreaming. We have many dreams during the night but at best only remember one or two upon awakening. Scientists think dreams are one way of dealing with psychological issues that you are dealing with.

Sleep deprivation is one of the ways we study sleep. Without sleep, your coordination, mental acuity, muscle, and skin tone all deteriorate. Naps have been found to be beneficial to make up for lost sleep. Just tell your boss that you're trying to be a better employee when he catches you napping. After all, sleep is important.

FIVE: TECHNOBABBLE

Men love technology. It's wonderful and frustrating at the same time. Using a digital video recorder (DVR) to skip commercials is absolutely fabulous. High-definition television allows you to see individual blades of grass on a putt at the Masters. MP3 players with ten thousand songs are technological wonders. Best of all, I can hide my musical tastes from others. No longer can my buddies see that I own all of Barry Manilow's music.

Many men love to become technogeeks. We stare at the old VCR as it blinks 12:00 but will gladly spend all Saturday to install an eight-speaker, digitally tuned, stereo-surround system to shake the entire neighborhood while watching movies. We love technology if it is neat, new, expensive, and takes a day to program.

We will dive into all the devices that let us proudly say "I am a tech-nogeek." Which is better: LCD screens or plasma screens? How do they make 3D movies? Can you use a cell phone in a metal building? How does sound surround you? And how do DVRs allow us to skip commercials? Turn off that 84-inch flat screen and let's examine the world of technology.

HOW DOES THE
INTERNET WORK?

The Internet owes its start to the Cold War. The U.S. Department of Defense initially funded a project in the late 1960s
to provide a reliable means of communication in the event of
a nuclear war. The project was designed to link the massive
computers of the day. Today, the Internet is a large-scale group
of networked computers, routers, dedicated information lines,
and phone lines that speed information around the globe.

You can think of the Internet as a worldwide highway system. The dedicated information lines are like superhighways.
These large information lines can handle trillions of cars
(messages) per second. They interconnect towns, countries,
and even continents. The routers are exits on and off of this
information superhighway to smaller roads (phone lines and
cable lines) that lead to your computer. Just like your house
has an address, so does your computer. This Internet Proto-
col (IP) address allows you to send a message to another IP
address and get a return response. And the best part is that
the messages can be sent almost at the speed of light—300
hundred million meters per second—right to your door.

An IP address is a major shortcut that makes the Internet
much easier to surf. It is really just a set of numbers, but it
can be replaced with a name like *www
.bobbymercerbooks.com*, which is
much easier to remember than
a string of numbers. You pay
an Internet service provider
(ISP) for access to your local
road and then you can surf
for hours.

> **Scientifically Speaking**
>
> Science is a wonderful
> thing, if you don't have to
> earn a living at it.
>
> —Albert Einstein

HOW ARE 3D MOVIES MADE?

Most three-dimensional movies use two separate cameras, each filming from a slightly different angle, but some newer ones create a second angle using computers. Couple two different pictures with a few filters and you are on your way to ducking as a dinosaur lunges at you. If you take off the glasses, the picture appears fuzzy because the images are slightly off-center.

Each camera lens is outfitted with a polarizing lens oriented in a different direction. Polarizing filters only allow one direction of light waves to pass through. The left lens may be up-and-down polarized, while the right lens is side-to-side polarized. The key is watching it with the ever-so-cool 3D glasses.

The glasses each have a polarized lens that is aligned with the lenses used in filming. Two cameras project the film onto the screen, and the polarizing filters allow only one scene to reach each eye. Your brain stacks those images up and sees in three dimensions. Many 3D movies from the 1950s used uber-cool red and green glasses to filter the two images, but today most 3D glasses use polarized lenses. The glasses make great sunglasses and create a fashion statement at the same time. Don't throw out the old red-green ones either, since a few video gaming systems are rumored to use them for newer games. Your optometrist could even put the lenses in stylish frames to improve the gaming experience. You won't play any better, but you will look better as you lose.

Scientifically Speaking

If it weren't for electricity we'd all be watching television by candlelight.

—George Gobel

HOW DOES A PLASMA TV WORK?

All light is created in an atom in the same manner. Electrons circle the atom in clouds at different layers; when they are excited by heat or electricity, a few of these electrons jump to a higher level. Think about walking to the top of a water slide, and when you slide down you let out a giant yell. For electrons, jumping up is like climbing that giant ladder. These excited electrons soon get bored and plunge back to their previous level. As they fall, they give off a photon of light, like your yell as you plunge.

Plasma TVs use plasma, which is electrically excited gas. Gases start neutral but can become charged as their electrons are ripped free from their host atoms. Free electrons are negative, and the old host atom is now positive. The net charge overall is still neutral, but you have shifted charges. To rip away these electrons, you need extreme heat or extreme electricity. Think of a plasma display screen as thousands of tiny fluorescent lights. Each pixel or point on the screen is composed of subpixels of red, green, and blue. By varying the intensity of those colors, you can create every color except black. To create black, just dial all the subpixels to zero.

The screen uses thousands of tiny glass cells full of a mixture of xenon and neon. When the cell is excited, it emits an invisible ultraviolet (UV) photon which strikes a red, green, or blue phosphor, which emits a visible photon. Each cell is excited by electricity delivered to an address electrode for each cell. The cells are excited several times a second, and the picture moves seamlessly.

Brain Fart

Sneezing onto your monitor will help you see the individual pixels, since the snot will act like a little magnifying glass.

HOW DOES AN LCD SCREEN WORK?

LCD stands for liquid-crystal display. The term *liquid crystal* is a bit misleading, because liquid crystals are not actually liquid but solids. However, the molecules in these crystals behave as a liquid, hence their name. Having a liquidlike appearance while actually being solid gives them the advantages of both.

LCD screens require small electric currents to manipulate the passage of light through the liquid-crystal molecules that act as a screen. The current causes the crystals to twist and let varying amounts of light through. LCD screens do not produce their own light; they just let you see existing light. Think of it like a bunch of windows opening and closing to create the picture on the screen.

The liquid-crystal display is sandwiched between polarized glass sheets, which are perpendicularly aligned to manipulate the intensity of light as it passes through the crystals. This allows it to quickly switch from displaying light images to dark images and the gray in between.

> **Did You Know?**
>
> To see polarization of light, just break apart your favorite sunglasses. Stack the lenses and rotate one to see what happens. As you rotate the lenses over each other, you will see complete darkness when they are perpendicular to each other.

Active-matrix displays are used to enhance the picture. These displays use transistors and capacitors in a matrix, which is located on the display glass. Electrical charges are sent to particular subpixels. LCD screens create color by using subtraction. They use filters to block out all of the colors except red, green, or blue for each subpixel. By varying the intensity on each subpixel they can create millions of colors. By actively manipulating electrical charges, you will see a sharper and clearer display on your television screen.

WHICH IS BETTER: LCD OR PLASMA?

There are advantages and disadvantages to each. The technology is changing so fast that it is hard to even keep up with the changes. You can be guaranteed that six months after you buy a new technology a better one will be available.

Plasma screens are extremely bright and deliver very sharp pictures from almost any angle. They can be very big and very thin, but many have limited life spans and use a ton of energy to power each individual electrode. LCD screens are flatter, can be hooked directly to a computer, and use less energy than a plasma screen, but they are often difficult to see at angles.

Advances in technology have almost made this question a tossup. Five years ago, plasma TVs were superior, but today there's not much difference. Now it is completely a personal and budgetary choice. But don't buy a particular type on my recommendation. You really should go to the store and buy a TV based on the recommendation of a pimple-faced teenager.

Did You Know?

The first televised sports broadcast—a college game between Columbia University and Princeton University—took place on May 17, 1939. Bet no one watched it on a plasma!

WHY WILL YOU MISS YOUR OLD TV?

Flat-screen televisions will be the wave of the future, but there will be one reason to miss your old cathode-ray tube (CRT). That reason is the raspberry effect. Stare at a CRT, then stick out your tongue and give it a good old raspberry. Cool, the screen will wobble. This trick won't work with your flat screen.

Who knew blowing a raspberry could be so much fun? Playing a saxophone (or most other instruments) can also create the same effect when you stare at the screen. Chomping Girl Scout cookies at a high rate of speed will also do it, but blowing a raspberry is cheaper. Girl Scout cookies cost more per pound than filet mignon, but we buy them anyway.

The raspberry effect works because your eyeballs are shaking. The screen refreshes sixty times per second in the United States, maybe fifty times per second in other countries, due to alternating electrical current. In other words, sixty times a second the screen turns on and off. Because your eye is moving, it is in a different position as the screen is drawn. As the image of the screen traces a path across your retina, it looks like the screen is moving. You can get the same effect by blowing a raspberry at most LED displays, like the red numbers on an alarm clock or many fluorescent lights.

Next time you are at work, walk around the office blowing raspberries at all of the electronic devices. Go ahead and do it. Your coworkers will love you!

Scientifically Speaking

Magnetism, as you recall from physics class, is a powerful force that causes certain items to be attracted to refrigerators.

—Dave Barry

HOW DOES A DVR PAUSE LIVE ACTION TELEVISION?

Digital video recorders (DVRs) are just a hard drive that your television signal is routed through. The signal is recorded into a television buffer any time the TV is on. Most of the buffers are one hour, which means that one hour of what you are watching is always being recorded. If you walk into the room fifteen minutes late, you can rewind and finish watching the movie from the start. The DVR just keeps recording the same channel. The best part is you can catch up by fast-forwarding by the commercials.

Pausing live action is probably the most advertised part of the system. You can pause while you go get grub. When you get back, you can pick up where you left off.

Most units allow you to record one channel while watching another, and a few even allow you to record two channels while watching a third. However, once the hard drive is full, you need to buy a new unit or download the information to a larger hard drive. I feel confident that the units will soon be integrated with your computer, but there is still a limited hard-drive space. Burning onto DVDs is a possible option.

One benefit of a DVR is the search feature that allows you to search by actor, show, keywords, and so on. You can record all of the great kung fu movies that run in the night by recording any title that contains the word *dragon*. This feature is great for practical jokes. You can set a DVR to record everything containing the word *Jesus* for an atheist friend. Or record everything starring Keanu Reeves for your friend in drama school. Just wipe your fingerprints off the remote if you try a prank.

HOW DOES SOUND
SURROUND YOU?

Surround sound is a given for today's technogeek and just about any movie fanatic. Surround sound specifically refers to the process developed by Dolby, but we commonly apply it to any multichannel system. Once the purview of moviegoers, surround sound is now fairly common in home theater setups. But getting sound to surround you has taken many years.

One of the earliest movies to use surround sound was *Fantasia* by Disney in 1940. The sound editor took separate recordings of each orchestra section and combined them in a fairly new way. He recorded tracks for each of four different speakers for the theater. Mostly by fading one orchestra section into another, he made the classical music surround the moviegoer by moving the sound around the theater.

Surround sound continued in smaller leaps until the 1970s. The Dolby Stereo system became the staple for theaters, and this is still pretty similar to what we use today. *Star Wars* was one of the earliest movies to use this technology. By fading music from the rear to the front speakers, moviegoers felt like the ships were flying right by them. The battles seemed to come alive. The rear speakers were used for background noise and moving spaceships. The front three speakers contained all of the dialogue. In theaters, a person talking on the left of the screen will come from the left speaker and so on.

In the 1980s surround sound came to our house and never left. The ability to simulate the movie theater experience was amazing. And we didn't have to take out a loan to buy a drink and stale popcorn. Fresh popcorn, cheap drinks, surround sound, and pausing the movie while we pee caused home-theater use to explode.

The earliest home theaters came with four separate recordings: track A, track B, the common parts of A and B, and the differences in A and B. Track A went to the left speaker, and track B went to the right speaker. The common parts of A and B went to the center-channel speaker. The different parts allow the front and rear speakers to play different sounds for each side of the room. The surround decoder lowers the volume for the rear speakers and adds the desired time delay. A variety of settings allow you to mimic an arena-sized venue or a quaint theater.

The subwoofer plays the low notes to shake the entire room. Low sounds cause your body, the chairs, and your walls to shake. Sound is just air pressure shaking your walls, kind of like miniature sonic booms. Low, loud sounds have the biggest difference in air pressure. These low notes cause the room to shake and us to love action movies. Romantic comedies are fine for single-speaker television sets, but guys want action. We want to feel the explosion. We want to duck as a light saber slices above our head. So we pay the money and spend four or five frustrating hours to set up our home theater. But we do it gladly, just to shake the entire house as we watch our favorite flick.

Scientifically Speaking

All of physics is either impossible or trivial. It is impossible until you understand it, and then it becomes trivial.

—Ernest Rutherford

WHAT ARE THE BENEFITS OF MP3S?

MP3 players have been a staple since the late 1990s. And why not? You can fit 20,000 songs on one little player, and nobody has to see that you have Celine Dion's music on auto shuffle.

MP3 files are compressed audio files, and there are several benefits to compressing an audio file. One, you can store more songs on a player. Two, you can download and upload them to the Internet quicker. The music loses almost nothing to the untrained ear.

MP3 players can be solid state or use a computer minidrive. Solid-state players have no moving parts, so they won't skip while you are exercising or in the car. Mini hard drives are usually loaded with built-in shock absorbers to prevent skipping. At the heart of the player is a microprocessor. You direct it to load a playlist that you previously created, and you are ready to play. The processor grabs the digital file from the memory and decodes it into an analog signal to drive the speakers in the ear buds. Most cars and home stereos are now outfitted to play MP3 files, but you can, of course, hook it up to an external amplifier to hear on more powerful speakers.

No CD cases littering your passenger seat. Nobody has to see your musical taste unless you want them to. Great for now, but MP3 players will soon be replaced by something smaller and faster. Trust me, your children will eventually look at you and laugh when you say you had an MP3 player. My students laugh when I talk about vinyl records. In a few years, kids will own MP37 players that contain every song ever recorded by every artist ever and double as an earring.

> **Did You Know?**
>
> MP3 is only one of several shrinking audio files, but it's the most popular at the moment. In a few years, it will probably be replaced with something smaller and faster.

HOW DOES AN IPHONE TOUCHSCREEN WORK?

The Apple iPhone took the market by storm. The simple flat black box came alive with the slide of a finger, but sales took off because of the touch of two fingers. The touch screen on the new phone was better than its predecessors. The two-finger pinch to resize pictures and graphics is the epitome of technocool.

Most touch screens use resistive technology. Two thin glass or plastic sheets compress when touched. The screen knows where your finger is located because the compression changes the resistance of a thin metal sheet. However, the iPhone goes above and beyond and uses capacitive technology.

Tiny capacitors located behind the screen can locate your finger even if it doesn't touch the screen. By aligning an array of thousands of tiny capacitors, the phone can determine the location of two fingers, and that is the secret to its success. Your body is a giant source of electric charge, and capacitors transfer electrons to store that charge. One plate becomes positive due to lack of electrons, and the other plate becomes negative due to the presence of extra electrons. As your fingertip approaches the screen, the plate will detect the location of your finger due to an increased capacitance.

Touch screens are now found only on high-end products, but soon they will be everywhere. Touch computer screens may replace the traditional mouse and touchpad soon. And as the technology gets better, we may even replace the traditional keyboard with a touch screen.

Scientifically Speaking

Somewhere, something wonderful is waiting to be known.

—Carl Sagan

HOW DO CELL PHONES WORK?

Cell phones are just a high-tech version of the walkie-talkie my parents would never buy me as a kid. The cell phone converts your speech into an electromagnetic radio wave by a process called superposition. Essentially, your audio wave superimposes itself on a carrier signal. The signal is sent to a cell tower that boosts the signal and sends it to the recipient. The recipient's cell phone subtracts off the carrier signal and converts the audio track back into audible sound.

In the early days of cell phones, the total number of cell areas was small and the phones were gigantic. Now phones are tiny and virtually the entire world is covered by at least one cell area. Cell phones allow us to be in contact with almost anyone in the world, which can be a good or a bad thing. So if you need to avoid a call, read the next question for a great excuse.

Brain Fart

Early cell phones were the size of a New York City phonebook. Try fitting that in your back pocket!

CAN YOU USE A CELL PHONE IN A METAL BUILDING?

You are out shopping at a big superstore and see the bargain of the century. You pull out your cell phone to make a call but can't get a reliable signal. Why? Any building that has a pre-dominantly metal shell will block most cell phone signals. The metal building acts like a Faraday cage. Michael Faraday theorized that electromagnetic, or e/m, waves would travel around a hollow conducting cage. Lo and behold, he was right.

The e/m waves cause electrons in the metal to move in response to them, and no waves can penetrate (or escape). The longer the wavelength, the easier it is to shield. Many early cell phones wouldn't even work in reinforced concrete buildings because the rebar acted like a Faraday cage. As long as the holes in the cage are smaller than the wavelengths that need to be blocked, the cage doesn't even have to be solid. For example, the metal screen inside a microwave door allows you to see in, but it also keeps the microwaves inside the oven, like a Faraday cage.

Newer cell phones are harder to shield because they use shorter wavelengths. Another way to help cell phone signals is to place an external antenna that connects to an internal antenna. Even in normal buildings, the cell phone signal will degrade as it passes through more solid materials. That is the reason you see all of those dorky-looking people walking around with their phones held in the air searching for a signal. If that doesn't work, try hopping on one leg as you hold the phone skyward.

Scientifically Speaking

"Darn, I lost an electron."
"Are you sure?"
"Yeah, I'm positive."

HOW DO THEY KNOW TO CHANGE A MOVIE REEL IN A THEATER?

Theater films are shipped in two to six reels of film for convenience. The amount of film required for a single feature would fill a reel over a meter (a little over a yard) across, so the film is cut into small segments to ship it. The term *cue marks* is given to the small oval that appears in theater movies. The next time you go to the movies, look for the oval. If you see it, you'll know it's time to change the reel. The cue marks are designed to help older theaters show the film, which have two cameras aimed at the screen. As a reel is about to end, the film is marked with an oval in the upper right corner. The oval signals the projectionist to turn one camera off and turn the other one on. Many theaters can now do it automatically. You see a seamless movie. Today theater technology is getting better. Many theaters now splice all the reels together onto one large horizontal reel before it is ever shown. The cue marks will probably show up, but they serve no purpose.

With the advent of digital theater projection, cue marks are going to disappear. Most movies will soon be coming to a theater near you over the computer, which means no shipping costs for the studio. The theater just downloads the film and stores it on the manager's hard drive. The film is then projected digitally onto the screen. The manager will be able to hit play from his or her office, so a projectionist will no longer be needed. I see all of the savings adding up. Ticket prices will go down and you won't have to take out a second mortgage to buy stale popcorn and a bladder-busting soda. Wow, I'm so glad the movie studios are finally trying to save me money.

WHAT IS THE BEST WAY TO FIX ELECTRONIC DEVICES?

From the first days of electronics, we have been frustrated with glitches. Our television picture would have an annoying scroll, or our radio's volume would change periodically. As three-year-olds we learned that if we hit malfunctioning things they might work again. For my toys as a kid, this method worked like a charm. It didn't work with my brother, but that is another story.

I had an early computer screen that would randomly vaporize into a single line, and after a good whack to the front it was good as new. This worked because old CRT tubes used an electron gun and a set of electromagnets to steer the stream of electrons. As the CRTs aged, the gun or electromagnets could eventually move. A good slap sometimes put them back in place.

Experts have a name for this—percussive maintenance. Experts have names for everything. A good sharp whack and many electronic glitches clear right up. The science of percussive maintenance is thin. Yes, electronic connections do become loose, and occasionally a good sharp slap will clear the problem. Even better than that, it makes us feel better. My computer wouldn't always come back until it had a few good slaps, but I felt better emotionally.

In a completely unscientific vein, I also found out that cussing while slapping the monitor made me feel better. Percussive maintenance will void the warranty of most major electronic devices, so never tell anyone at the store that you tried that before you returned it. It might be better to wait until the device is out of warranty and then slap away.

SIX: PARTY TIME TIPS AND TRICKS

Men enjoy a good party. We enjoy the sights, sounds, and all the other distractions created by people having fun. Whether we are at a pub or a cookout in our own backyard, we love hanging out with friends. As we age, we drink more responsibly (or not at all), and we still have a good time. College parties may be a distant memory, but they are probably a pleasant memory.

Most of us have a few great party stories from our youth. My favorite party words were "Hey, watch this." When I heard them, I knew something really outlandish was coming. I imagine more partygoers have been hurt by those words than any others. Luckily, I never said them—at least not that I remember. Now that I am older, when a friend utters those words, I make him explain what he is going to do beforehand. If it's safe, I let him go ahead.

Bar bets, floating kegs, and breathalyzers are all-time party staples, but the science of a party is also amazing. Have you ever wondered why ice sinks in bourbon? Or why tequila won't freeze? Belly up to the bar and let's take a look at the science of parties.

WHY DO KEGS FLOAT?

Kegs are large cylinders with a central flow pipe and a valve that allows gases out. Kegs come in different sizes and are a party staple around the world. The standard U.S. keg is 15.5 gallons of that glorious liquid that gives men the courage to ask women out. The standard U.K. keg is 50 L (about 13 gallons), and you can buy pony kegs (7.75 gallons) and mini kegs (1.3 gallons) as well. You can store other liquids in kegs, but beer is the hands-down favorite. Beer stored in a keg is pasteurized, pressurized, and will stay fresh longer, at least until you try to float it in a container of ice.

Objects float because of buoyancy—an upward force caused by the pressure from the liquid around the object. Even air, defined as a fluid due to its ability to flow, gives you a small buoyant force. If you jump in a pool you'll feel a greater buoyant force than you would by walking in because the water pressure will be greater. Basically, the water is trying to push in on all sides of you. Since the water pressure at the bottom of your body is greater than at the top of your body, you are pushed upwards. Gravity pushes you down, and the buoyant force pushes you up. When you stand on the ground, gravity wins because the buoyant force from air is so small. In a pool, the buoyant force is usually equal to the force of gravity (weight) and you float.

A keg, usually made from aluminum, starts out full of that wonderful liquid pressurized with carbon dioxide (just like sodas). Most party hosts will place the keg in a gigantic tub of ice water to keep the beer cold. The keg will sink to the bottom because the keg and that frothy liquid combine for a great

Brain Fart

A full size keg is supposed to contain about 165 glasses of beer at twelve ounces a pop. Go ahead and count them at your next keg party. Good luck keeping up!

weight. Gravity wins! Tapping the keg allows the beer to flow. Most parties use a party pump, which allows air in as the beer flows out. As the partygoers drink away, air replaces the liquid. The weight of the keg gets smaller by the glass. Eventually the weight equals the buoyant force and the keg floats! This will usually be met with cheers of adulation, but the work isn't done yet. Most kegs may still only be half drained at that point.

Density and buoyancy go hand in hand. Density is the mass per unit volume of any material. Buoyancy is the upward force on an object caused by differing densities. When you "kill" a keg, you are adding air to it, which decreases the mass and therefore the density. As soon as the density of the keg is equal to the water's density, the keg floats.

Floating a keg takes dedication, desire, a big bladder, and lots of friends. You can float one even easier in salt water, which supplies a greater buoyant force. So next time you have a kegger, you may want to head for the beach. To learn more about buoyancy, let's switch to the hard stuff and learn about ice in bourbon.

WHY DOES ICE SINK IN A GLASS OF BOURBON?

Ice floats in liquid water. This is the opposite of what you would expect. Solids are typically denser than their liquid counterparts and therefore sink when added to a liquid. This doesn't happen with water because as the liquid water cools to near freezing (4°C or 39°F), the water's density changes. At this point, the molecules move very slowly and are attracted to each other. However, as they group together, they bond into organized hexagonal patterns. This is the most efficient way of packaging water molecules. When water forms these hexagonal patterns, there is empty space between the molecules, which makes the frozen water less dense than the liquid form. In this case, water's solid form takes up more space (less dense) than the liquid form. Thus, solid water floats in liquid water. Water is the only common substance to do this.

When we add the same ice to bourbon (or almost any alcohol), it sinks to the bottom of the glass because the density of alcohol is less than the density of the ice. Bartenders can even make cool layered drinks based on the differing densities of types of alcohol. This also helps because as the ice melts the water stays on the bottom, and your drink doesn't get watered down. I took advantage of this when I was a wee lad by stealing some of my dad's bourbon and pouring water back in. The top layer would be pure bourbon, and he was none the wiser. Until he finished the bottle! Luckily, he drank slowly. I was of legal age before he finished.

Scientifically Speaking

Nothing in life is to be feared. It is only to be understood.

—Marie Curie

WHAT IS THE SECRET TO LAYERED DRINKS?

Striped drinks of different colors are great conversation starters. They are carefully prepared, only to be slammed down in one gulp most of the time, but what is the secret to this alcoholic art?

The secret is density. All alcohol has a proof number, which gives the percentage of alcohol. Eighty proof has 40 percent alcohol and 60 percent water and some form of sugar. A general rule of thumb is the higher the proof, the lower the density. Density causes all objects to sink. Vinegar sinks in oil because the vinegar's density is greater than that of oil. A good shake will mix them up, but they will eventually settle back out.

To make a layered drink, pour the densest liquid in the shot glass first. For the next layers, a spoon will help. Turn the spoon over and gently pour the next liquid onto the back of the spoon. Continue layering until the drink is done. Now pass out the rounds and slam them away. The liquors mix in your mouth and burn on the way down. With different colored alcohols, it is possible to make any variety of colors. You can even make my favorite, the Buttery Nipple.

Did You Know?

You can even show off patriotic drinks like the Red, White, and Blue (grenadine, peach schnapps, and blue curaçao); the Irish Flag (crème de menthe, Irish cream liqueur, and Grand Marnier); or the Mexican Flag (grenadine, crème de menthe, and tequila).

WHAT IS THE SECRET TO CRUSHING A BEER CAN ON YOUR FOREHEAD?

Crushing a can takes strength, speed, and inertia. Inertia is the resistance to a change in motion of an object. The more massive an object is, the more inertia it has. Your head is massive (at least when compared to the can). You grab one end of the can and violently smash it into your forehead. Your head's inertia will want to keep it stationary. The can's smaller inertia will cause it to change shape. Just think about it; you wouldn't crush a keg into your forehead. It also helps to have a Cro-Magnon forehead and a really hard head. Harder heads have more inertia and fewer brains.

There are far better ways to see the same concept. Take a brick and the same beer can. Place the can on the ground and drop the brick onto it. The can will crush because of inertia. The brick has more mass and wants to keep moving, so it crushes the can. This is a much smarter way to get cans ready for the recycling bin. Leave forehead can-crushing to guys named Hammerhead.

Brain Fart

Most people who crush a can on their forehead regret it the next morning. Most cans crushed on the forehead are beer cans. Coincidence? I think not.

WHY DOES THE FALLING DOLLAR TRICK WORK?

The falling bill trick is a fun way to win a free drink. There is no better word than *free*. You pay zip, nothing, nada. And you can give a little science lesson as you drink that free ale.

Here's the setup: Hold a dollar bill by your fingertips with the dollar bill hanging down to the floor. Have your opponent place his or her thumb and forefinger around the center of the bill but not touching it. Bet him he can't catch it two out of three times as you drop it. If your opponent has been drinking, you can probably bet that he won't catch it any of the drops.

The science behind this trick is reaction time and falling bodies. As an object falls, gravity is the primary force responsible for its acceleration. All objects accelerate at 9.8 meters per second every second (that's 32 feet per second every second) near the Earth's surface (if you ignore air resistance). Since the bill is perpendicular to the floor, air resistance is not much of a factor. The average human reaction time is 0.15 seconds. That is the time between when you see something and your brain can get a message to the muscles. And, of course, reaction time will be slowed if alcohol is involved.

> **Did You Know?**
>
> No piece of paper money can be folded more than seven times. Go ahead and try.

According to physics, the bill will fall over 11 cm in that same time. Half of a U.S. dollar bill is 8 cm in length, so someone attempting to grab it will just miss the bill. If you use non-U.S. currency, check the dimensions first. Two out of three is a safe bet, since occasionally someone will time the drop correctly. The bill falls to the floor and you win free stuff (or a few coins).

You can also show that you have better reaction times than your opponent by dropping the bill with one hand while you catch it with your other hand. You are just so amazing! Be careful not to do this trick in a room full of Olympic athletes, since they probably have exceptional reflexes (reaction time). You might want to steer clear of hardcore video game players also, since they spend thousands of hours improving their reaction time.

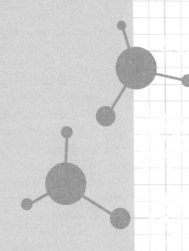

WHAT IS THE SECRET TO THE UPSIDE-DOWN SHOT GLASS?

The classic upside-down shot glass has been done by countless bar patrons over the years. This is also the perfect trick to amaze your six-year-old nephew. The needed supplies are readily available, and the trick always works. Take a shot glass and fill it up with water. Of course, you can always use your favorite liquor, but not with your six-year-old nephew. Matter of fact, you might want to use a regular drinking glass for him. You don't want him going home and saying "Look what Uncle John showed me with a shot glass." You might lose serious points in the family game.

Take your full shot glass and place your driver's license over the open top. A playing card or any flat, rigid, nonporous surface will work. Press down slightly on the card and turn the drink over while pressing. Release the card and the liquid magically floats upside down. Make sure you line up any bets or payoffs before you turn it over. Your amazing abilities have allowed you to defy gravity.

Make sure you never try this trick in space. The trick will somewhat work, but you will eventually have round drops of liquor floating around your spaceship. Floating around and slurping up the liquor might be fun, so maybe you should actually try this on your next junket into orbit.

The trick works because of air pressure. Air pushes on us from all sides and is actually trying to rush into the space that our body occupies. When you flip the glass over, the water is pushing down, but the air pressure is pushing up. The air pressure wins. And maybe you win too.

> **Did You Know?**
>
> You can't hard-boil an egg on Mt. Everest because of air pressure. Lower air pressure causes the boiling point to be much lower (about 70°C or 158°F) than at or near sea level, so while you can boil the water, it's not hot enough to hard-boil the egg.

HOW DO YOU TRADE WHISKEY FOR WATER?

How about a new classic bar bet. Trading whiskey for water is sure to be a hit at your next party. This trick is definitely not recommended for your six-year-old nephew. Adults only, please. Take two shot glasses. Fill one completely with whiskey (or bourbon). Fill the other with water. Place a driver's license over the shot of water, then invert it and carefully place over the whiskey shot. Slowly slide the card out until you have a tiny opening between the two glasses. Sit back, watch, and enjoy.

You will see the dark liquor slowly travel toward the top. It will take at least a minute for the process to finish. With practice, you can even invert the whiskey shot with the card slightly off center, but you have to get it back down on the water shot fast.

The trick isn't a trick at all; it is simple physics. Whiskey has a lower density than water, so it will gradually float to the top. This trick will also work with vodka and gin. Try it. I dare you. Just let me know when it is done.

Brain Fart

Trading whiskey for water is just like Italian dressing separating in the bottle, but Italian dressing won't impress your friends.

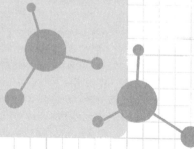

HOW DO YOU PICK UP AN ICE CUBE WITH A PIECE OF HAIR?

Pulling hair got you into trouble as a kid. Now you can use that previously frowned upon skill to fill up your bank account. The best part is your sister will no longer go rushing to your mom to tattle on you. Not only can you win cash with this, but you'll be viewed as the coolest uncle or dad on the planet.

The supplies for this trick are also easy to come by. All you need is a long hair (or thread), a salt shaker, and a cube of frozen water. If male pattern baldness runs in your family, opt for the thread. Lay the hair across the ice cube. Sprinkle a little salt on the cube over the hair. Wait about thirty seconds and lift the cube by the hair. Your victims will be amazed and astounded. If you wagered, collect your winnings. If it was a family show, bask in the adulation of being the coolest family member on the planet. You might want to practice in private before you make any wagers.

> **Did You Know?**
>
> Saturn would float on water since its density is less than that of H_2O (one g/mL).

The trick works because salt lowers the freezing point of water and causes some of the ice to melt. This is the reason that salt trucks are used in the winter on icy roads.

The melted water will wash away some of the salt and the ice will refreeze, trapping the hair and allowing you to pick up the cube.

Using salt to lower the freezing point of water is also the reason you use salt mixed with ice in homemade ice cream recipes. It lowers the temperature of the cream to below the freezing point so you can eat that summer treat.

HOW DO BEER FUNNELS WORK?

The competitive nature of guys led to the invention of the beer funnel. Luckily, this is fun that we grow out of later in life. It's cute at a party at the age of twenty-two but incredibly sad at thirty. Beer funnels are definitely for the twenty-one- to twenty-nine-year-old demographic. A single bottle or can of beer is okay in a funnel, but any more than that is not safe.

The science of the beer funnel is pretty simple. Attach a hose to a funnel and fill up the funnel with beer. You need to use your thumb to hold the torrent of suds back until you are ready. Put the hose in your mouth as you pull the thumb away. The suds rush down into your mouth due to gravity and air pressure.

The secret is the elevated funnel. It creates a pressure head. The pressure comes from the potential energy stored in the conical reservoir and the air pushing on the exposed liquid. Air pressure and gravity push the beer down into your mouth. A beer funnel is no different than chugging a beer. Except if you quit a beer funnel, you get covered in beer. Chugging allows you to just tip the can toward the ground when you can't finish.

The first beer funnels were created in the Middle Ages as a great party pleaser. A half pint of grog was added to a goatskin funnel and away they went. A few hundred years later, a scientist was at a party and a light bulb went off. Well, at least a metaphorical light bulb went off, since electricity hadn't yet been harnessed. A giant beer funnel would be the perfect way to avoid trips to the well for water.

Water towers are the perfect way to deliver water right to your doorstep, and these follow the same principle as the beer funnel. Put a giant water tower in town and connect hoses to each house. The owner of the house could just open a valve and the water would flow freely. Before the advent of large pumps, this was the gold standard for in-home water delivery. And just think, we owe that water tower to a goatskin full of grog and three or four buddies cheering the drinker on.

WHAT CAUSES THE DONALD DUCK HELIUM EFFECT?

Inhaling helium is dangerous. It can kill you. NEVER suck helium from a pressurized cylinder. You can pass out within a minute and die. A single shallow breath from a balloon is okay, but no more. And make sure you breathe normally for several minutes before trying it again.

Okay, warning over! So how does a single shallow breath change your voice? It changes because of the helium (duh). But let's understand how you make sounds in the first place. Your lungs push air up the larynx, and the air vibrates the vocal cords as it rushes out. By moving your mouth, tongue, and lips, you create spoken words or songs. By repeating what you hear, you eventually learn how to create the sounds you want.

You even create a few sounds that you may not want. That is the reason for crazy accents; you mimic what you hear all the time. Most areas in the world have their own unique accents. As guys, we laugh about accents, until we hear French girls talk, then we fall in love. They could read the phone book and we would be enchanted.

Brain Fart

Raise a baby in Boston and she will grow up saying "Pahk the cah in the yahd." Raise the kid in the southern United States and he will grow up "ahootin' and ahollerin'."

Spoken or sung sounds are created by a variety of resonant frequencies from the column of air created by your larynx and mouth. The lowest frequency is called the fundamental, and the higher frequencies are called overtones. The sum of all of the frequencies is the pitch and timbre (quality) that you hear.

Scientifically Speaking

The joy of discovery is the certainly the liveliest that the mind of a man can ever feel.

—Claude Bernard

In normal air, the fundamental frequency is the loudest. Helium is a lighter gas and allows the sound wave to travel faster. When you inhale helium, the gas moves faster, and sounds from the lower frequencies decrease in loudness, replaced by an increase in the higher overtones. The overall pitch doesn't change because your vocal cords are still vibrating the same since your body is trying to reproduce the same sound. The timbre changes because the overtones are amplified. Your voice sounds like Donald Duck.

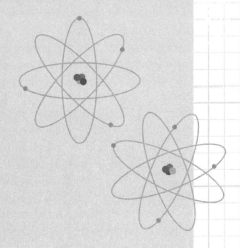

HOW DO BREATHALYZERS WORK?

Breathalyzer is actually a brand name that is now applied to an entire line of devices. You may find it ironic that the original Breathalyzers were created by the Smith and Wesson Company, although they were later sold to another company.

Breathalyzers are an easy way for the police to measure blood alcohol content (BAC) on the roadside. A urine test or a blood sample is more accurate, but most police officers don't like needles. And they darn sure wouldn't want you peeing on their shoes, so the breathalyzer was invented.

Alcohol is not digested as you drink it, nor is it chemically changed in the bloodstream. As blood passes through the lungs, some of the alcohol moves across the lung membranes into the air. The concentration of the alcohol in the air you breathe out is related to the concentration of the alcohol in the blood. As alcohol is exhaled, it can be detected by the device.

Modern breathalyzers use one of three different technologies: a color change, infrared spectroscopy, or a fuel cell. They all measure the alcohol level on your breath. Breath mints, garlic, and onions may change the odor of your breath, but they won't change your BAC. Mouthwash will change your BAC, but in the wrong way because most brands contain alcohol. Gargling to fool a cop is a bad idea. Let's examine the three types from the comfort of a chair. Do not try to read and drive at the same time; it's as dangerous as drinking and driving.

The original testing method used a chemical reaction to produce a color change. Your breath is bubbled through a solution of sulfuric acid, silver nitrate, and potassium dichromate. The sulfuric acid removes the alcohol from your breath into a liquid solution. The alcohol then reacts with the potassium dichromate to form potassium sulfate, chromium sulfate, vinegar, and water. The dichromate changes from a reddish brown color to a green color as it forms the chromium sulfate. More alcohol leads to a deeper green. The silver nitrate is just a catalyst that helps the process along and is unaffected, similar to the wingman concept when you are out at a party. To find out the BAC, a photocell shines light through the mix and compares to a control. The deeper the green, the more light that is absorbed and the bigger trouble the driver is in.

Another type of breath tester uses infrared or IR spectroscopy to find BAC. Ethyl alcohol is composed of carbon, hydrogen, and oxygen. The bonded oxygen-hydrogen is what makes it an alcohol. Almost all chemical bonds bend and stretch like a spring. This bending and stretching is what the device uses to find BAC. These molecules are continuously wiggling. The wiggling changes as the molecules absorb IR waves. IR light shines through a breath sample. The absorbed wavelength of IR tells the police if ethanol is present, and the amount absorbed tells the BAC.

Brain Fart

If life hands you a lemon, break out the tequila and salt!

The final type of breath tester uses fuel-cell technology. The device contains an electrolyte sandwiched between two platinum electrodes. As a breath is blown across one electrode, alcohol is oxidized to form vinegar, electrons, and protons. The electrons flow from one electrode to the other through an ammeter that measures the electrical current. A greater current means a greater BAC. Protons (naked hydrogen atoms) flow to the other side and join with oxygen to form water. You may get arrested, but you are creating much-needed energy for our world.

Breath testers must be calibrated and used correctly. The police often follow the breath test with a urine or blood sample. Home-use breath testers are more affordable than ever but aren't as reliable. Good thing my dad never had one of those.

WHY WON'T ALCOHOL FREEZE?

Many people keep a bottle of tequila stashed in the freezer for when the urge strikes. Frozen margaritas are also a party favorite, but why doesn't tequila freeze? It does freeze, just not at the temperature of your freezer. Ethanol is the alcohol in most types of liquor, and in its pure state it freezes at about -114°C (-173°F). Your freezer only goes down to about -4°C (25°F). By mixing water with the alcohol, the distillers raise the freezing point, but it is still below what your home freezer's reaches. Anything below 80 proof (40 percent alcohol) may freeze in your freezer.

Don't stash a six-pack of beer in the freezer or you may end up with busted bottles and ruptured cans. Beer and wine have a significantly lower level of alcohol content. The water in each may freeze and expand to crack the bottles. (See the next question for a neat exception to this rule.) Water is one of the only substances that grows as it freezes. Fish are glad for this fact. The ice on a lake will float to the top and allow the surface of the lake to freeze. This insulates the lake from further temperature drop. If, like most liquids, water shrank as it froze, the lake would fill up with ice from the bottom, and the little fishies would die when the lake froze solid. Fish would be permanently removed from the menu.

Next time you watch a frozen Philadelphia Eagles game in January, keep an eye on the crowd. The cameraman will find the guys that take their shirts off as they cheer. These intrepid fans lubricated their bloodstream with a little human anti-freeze and aren't going to die from hypothermia because their blood can no longer freeze. People will do anything to get on television.

HOW DO YOU FREEZE A BEER IN THIRTY SECONDS?

One of the greatest party tricks of all time is the frozen beer trick. You can see this trick best with beer in a clear bottle, like Corona. Place a full bottle of beer in a freezer for one to two hours. Pull the beer out of the freezer, and if it is still liquid, you are ready to start. Bang the bottom on a countertop and hand it to a friend. You can watch as the beer freezes in the bottle.

The beer will start freezing inside the top of the bottle, and you can watch as the ice crystals migrate down the bottle. Within thirty seconds your beer will be completely frozen. Luckily, the beer will thaw out and be perfectly normal.

By placing the bottle in the freezer, you are creating a supercooled fluid. Supercooled fluids are below the freezing point of the liquid, but they won't freeze without some additional agitation. The beer is under pressure due to the carbon dioxide in the liquid. It is below the freezing point of the water in the beer, but the water doesn't freeze because there are no nucleation points around which the ice crystals can form. When you bang the bottle on the table, you release some of the carbon dioxide, creating tiny bubbles. These bubbles are nucleation points and give the ice crystals a place to start. The ice will cascade down the bottle as new ice crystals form on the previous crystals.

The trick also works with most sodas, but it will ruin the taste. You will end up with a flat soda since the carbon dioxide is what gives it the fizz. You also end up with a flat beer, but you'll still drink it. No guy wastes beer. The beer will still taste okay because the amount of carbon dioxide in the beer is less than the amount in a soda. Word of warning: Sometimes the bottle will freeze in the freezer. This happens if the freezer or the beer gets bumped. Ice will form in the bottle and the bottle will break as the ice expands. But if you put the bottle in the freezer and leave it alone, you will have success.

The Frozen Beer Trick

Ice crystals form at the top around carbon dioxide bubbles.

POW

The ice crystals cascade down the bottle in less than a minute.

SEVEN: MR. FIX-IT

Before the birth of cable television, men would barter home-improvement chores. We would trade our carpentry skills for a friend's plumbing skills. Nobody even tried to have more than one skill, and our partners didn't ask (or expect) us to. Old-fashioned hardware stores were like kid's clubhouses; a giant sign saying "No Girls Allowed" was posted on the front door. The gigantic home-improvement warehouse stores were not in existence yet. Only real live professionals even knew where to find things like grout, Teflon tape, and circuit breakers.

The advent of cable television caused an abundance of do-it-yourself shows to pop up on the tube. It must be really easy to gut a bathroom, replace all the fixtures, and repaint. It only took the guy and the girl on the show thirty minutes, even with commercial breaks, and the hot girl on the show never even broke a sweat. I wish the remodeling shows actually showed everything that happens during a commercial break. Like the legions of experts that work during the breaks and the hot girl sitting in a director's chair getting her nails done.

Anyway, the gigantic warehouse stores must have been in league with the cable companies, because they now give us a place to buy grout, Teflon tape, and circuit breakers. And those stores even let girls in! Great! Now we have to change a whole countertop because the color just doesn't go with the new paint.

Back in the day, we would just figure out a way to live without something being fixed. A cracked toilet was fine as long as it didn't leak. If it leaked, we called a plumber or Uncle Fred, who was a plumbing expert. All walls were white because they only sold six colors of wall paint anyway. We never put a new plug on a lamp. We just avoided grabbing the cord where the bare wire showed through. Yep, the cable companies and warehouse stores are responsible for our home-improvement nightmares.

I know some people enjoy home-improvement projects, and this chapter is for them. We will cover the good, the bad, and the ugly of home-improvement science. I'll teach you the best ways to open a locked door, the best and worst reasons for doing projects, and much, much more. Grab your tool belt as we explore the science of home improvements.

HOW DO LOW-FLOW TOILETS WORK?

Doo-doo runs downhill, but it needs water to help it along. Low-flow toilets are designed to accomplish the feat with less water. They work for the average load, but the heavy work always demands a plunger. I personally think low-flow toilets were designed by the makers of plungers.

All toilets use water from the tank to flush into the bowl, which pushes the contents of the bowl down the drain line. The tanks on low-flow toilets hold less water (typically 1 gallon or 1.6 L) than older toilets (6 gallons or about 10 L). The two types of toilets work in a similar way, but toilet manufacturers have adapted the siphons on low-flow toilets for a smoother flow. This allows these low-flow toilets to use less water. This is good for the environment, but not always good for guys. For us, the big stuff sometimes gets trapped at the bottom of the siphon, and more water or a plunger is required. I am all for saving water, but using a plunger twice a day is no fun. The most reliable trick I know is holding down the handle, which allows all of the water in the tank to drain. But that won't always work for the big stuff.

> ### Brain Fart
>
> Low-flow toilets were definitely not designed for men.

Another way to save water in your house is to install a urinal for liquid work, but I have a better idea for a new and improved toilet. Build it with a dial scale (like on a guitar amp) for each flush: 1 for easy listening all the way to 10 for head-banging heavy metal. This would save water and take care of the dirty work at the same time. Of course, the plunger companies might buy up the patent to keep this invention hidden.

One toilet manufacturing company is already onto my idea. They have a dual-flush toilet with two buttons, 1 for liquids only and 2 for the heavy stuff. The lower setting uses less than one gallon, and the higher setting uses about 1.6 gallons. Using the numbers one and two is cute, but we need more choices. I still want a dial that goes from 1 to 10.

Now it is time for a bit of toilet trivia. The flush toilet was not invented by Thomas Crapper as widely assumed. Although he was a plumber of note in nineteenth-century England, the flush toilet was already in existence. He did put his company logo on all of the toilets he sold. Some people assume that *crapper* became slang in the United States for a toilet after GIs returned after seeing the Crapper name on so many English toilets. This actually may be complete crap, since the nickname was already used in England before that.

HOW HAS THE PLUNGER
IMPROVED IN THE LAST
FORTY YEARS?

Plungers are a valuable tool in today's world. With low-flow toilets now the norm, they are as needed as toilet paper. When heavy stuff fails to clear the siphon elbow, your trusty plunger can help save the day. The plunger seals the opening and allows you to plunge. Pushing down on the handle helps trapped water (and air) to push the offending material over the siphon elbow and down the pipes. Sometimes repeated plunging is needed.

An old plunger was simply a rubber hemisphere at the end of a stick, but new ones are improved with a narrower opening and corrugated sides. The narrower opening helps by using a fluid principle called the equation of continuity. This equation states that the product of area and speed will remain constant anywhere in a pipe. The smaller area means the trapped water must leave the plunger with a higher speed. And to a toilet expert, higher speed equals better plunging. The corrugated sides also help because they allow the plunger to collapse with a greater speed.

Scientifically Speaking

The voyage of discovery lies not in seeking new horizons but in seeing with new eyes.

—Marcel Proust

WHY DOES THE WIND CAUSE MY TOILET WATER TO MOVE?

On a windy day, if you close the door to your bathroom and look in the bowl, you'll see science at work. This is best done before you make a deposit, but it will happen either way. If the wind is whistling, you will see the water slosh around in the bowl.

Most single-family houses have a vent pipe that goes through the roof. Traditionally, this vent is uncapped and exposed to the elements. The pipe prevents sewer gas from backing up into your house. When the wind blows over the vent opening, the Bernoulli effect takes place. The effect says that high speed air results in areas of low pressure. The wind creates low pressure in the vent line. This causes the water in the vent line to rise because of the lower air pressure above it. Since this water is connected to what is in the toilet bowl, the water in the bowl will slosh around. Turns out that science is the perfect reason to take a look into the bowl!

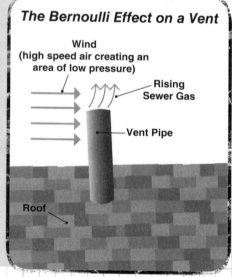

The Bernoulli Effect on a Vent

Wind
(high speed air creating an area of low pressure)

Rising Sewer Gas

Vent Pipe

Roof

HOW DOES A TANKLESS
WATER HEATER WORK?

Tankless water heaters are the wave of the future. They are smaller and more energy efficient than the large traditional units with tanks. Traditional water heaters use an electric heating element or a gas burner to keep a tank of hot water at a prescribed temperature. Tankless water heaters also use an electric heating element or a gas burner, but they heat the water directly in the pipe as it gets delivered to your faucet.

The new heaters are not instantaneous, but they can still deliver hot water faster than a tank heater because they can be placed closer to the faucet. Most traditional heaters are located in your garage or basement, but a tankless heater can be put almost anywhere. Larger houses will even have more than one tankless heater for increased demands. Tankless heaters only run when you demand the hot water, unlike the traditional style. You save energy by eliminating the passive heat loss you would have through the walls of the storage tank. Almost-instant hot water when you need it and savings on your energy bills make tankless water heaters the wave of the future.

Did You Know?

Balloons and rubber bands last longer when they are refrigerated.

HOW DO YOU PICK A LOCK?

Picking locks is another skill learned in movie action-hero school (along with hot-wiring cars and making gun silencers). I imagine spies are also taught this in spy school. I can tell you where I learned this, but I'll then have to kill you. It is an easy concept to understand but incredibly difficult to master.

We'll start with the basic pin-and-tumbler style lock, the most common lock in the world. The lock has a center core that connects to the bolt. The center core turns freely when the correct key is inserted, or when an expert picker is hard at work. The center core has three to seven pairs of pins that extend into the lock housing. The pin pairs rest atop each other, and each pair is held in place by tiny springs. The pins are different lengths corresponding to the ridges on your key. When the correct key is inserted, the bottom pin of the pair will just clear the cylinder and will rotate freely to open the lock.

Picking a lock takes at least two tools: a tension wrench and a lock pick. The tension wrench is just a thin L-shaped piece of metal designed to turn the core. The pick looks like a dentist tool, long and thin with a tiny hook on the end. Insert the wrench, twist the lock slightly, and maintain this tension. Slide the pick above the wrench and locate each pin. Attack the tightest pin first. Using the pick, press up on the pin until you feel it pop free. The pin will actually rest on the top of the slightly turned core. You should be able to twist the tension wrench a little more with each pin. Repeat until you have done all of the pins. The bolt will open.

You can pick a lock with a paper clip and a screwdriver, but only if you are a real-life action hero. Picking a lock also takes more time than they show in a movie, and the lock may be more complex. Most professional burglars have a set of lock picks, which are illegal to carry in most areas. Just be aware: Picking someone else's lock without their permission is illegal. You might want to start your life of crime by picking padlocks first, since they contain a smaller number of pins. Or for some locks you can try an even easier method.

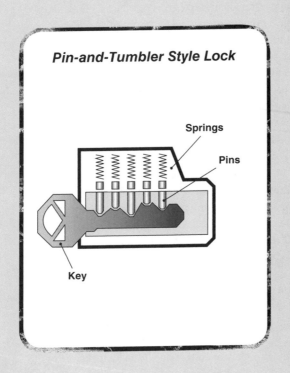

Pin-and-Tumbler Style Lock

Springs

Pins

Key

HOW DO YOU OPEN A DOOR WITH A CREDIT CARD?

This skill is also taught at movie action-hero school, but many of the students already know this before the class. I had an entire high school physics class that could open my classroom door with their student ID cards. One student taught everybody else how to do it. When I asked who opened it, they each pointed at the person sitting to their right. Luckily they were good kids. I sure hope criminals never figure out how to do this. I've said it before and I'll say it again: Make sure this book doesn't fall into the hands of anyone of questionable morals!

Be aware that opening a door with a credit card only works with certain locks. This method will not open a dead bolt. Also, this method can ruin credit cards. It's better to try this out with the fake ones that come with unwanted credit card offers. Push the door in as far as possible. Slide the card between the frame and the door knob directly in line with the bolt. Bend the card till it almost touches the door knob. Now bend the card toward the frame and open the door. This will work on many doors due to their design. The bolt is beveled, which allows you to close the door with the bolt out. The bevel helps the bolt recede into the door. By sliding in your credit card, you're actually pushing on the front of the bevel and pushing the entire bolt back.

Again, entering someone else's house is illegal unless you have permission, and some locks have an extra metal plate installed to foil this method. If the lock is backwards, you can cut a U shape in your credit card and pull the card to open it. By the way, if your doors open this easily, call a locksmith and get them fixed. Science has shown you at least two ways to get inside when you're locked outside. But there is a third way.

WHAT IS THE BEST WAY TO KICK IN A DOOR?

Kicking in a door should only be done in an emergency setting and only on your own door. There are a few rules that you must understand before you try to kick in a door.

1. Breaking and entering is illegal.
2. Try the door knob first and look for open windows.
3. Try picking the lock as previously shown.
4. Never try to kick in a metal door.
5. Always kick in the direction the door opens.
6. Call a locksmith, unless it is an emergency (or the director says "Action").
7. Always refer to rule #1.

Television cops make kicking in a door look so easy. And it is for them. They are actually sitting in a chair while a stunt double kicks in a balsa wood door. Most of us don't have a stunt double. We have to do our own door kicking.

The science of kicking a door in is fairly simple. Apply enough force until the doorjamb breaks. You can use a sidekick or a front kick, but always have your heel strike first. Kick through the door by aiming for a spot 30 centimeters on the other side of the door. Just like in golf, a good follow-through is essential. Aim right below the door knob or deadbolt. If it has a deadbolt, keep kicking. Eventually you will break the doorjamb and the door will open. Or you will break your foot and stop trying.

Actually, you should never do this in anger. It is far easier to call a friend who has a key or a locksmith. Even smarter would be to hide a key in those cute little fake rocks. On

second thought, scratch
the fake rock key holder
idea. Most of those
scream "I am a fake
rock key holder, please
burglarize my house!"
You might want to try the fake frog key
holder because those look much more realistic. Much wiser
would be to give the little old lady next door a key. She is
already keeping an eye on the comings and goings at your
place anyway.

HOW DO EPOXY GLUES WORK?

Epoxy is a two-part glue containing a resin and a hardener. The hardening agent in epoxy is a catalyst that causes the structure of the molecules to change. When the epoxy resin is mixed with the hardener, the molecules created are cross-linked and much stronger than traditional glue and even super glue. Time and heat are the major factors in getting the epoxy to cure, or set, the bond. These glues belong to a class of adhesives called structural adhesives.

Epoxy is used by model builders, car body repairmen, and even dentists. Dentists actually use an epoxy that hardens under the effect of ultraviolet light. The chemical reaction of the resin and hardener actually gives off heat in most instances to hurry the process along, important when someone has their hands in your mouth. A crown or new filling can be hardened in about thirty seconds by the high-powered backlight the dentist uses. Curing will usually take anywhere from two to twelve hours for a permanent bond. If you need a faster bond, try super glue or ask a dentist for help.

Did You Know?

Barbers were some of the first dentists and performed services such as tooth extraction, drilling, and filling cavities.

HOW DOES SUPER GLUE WORK?

Super glue is truly super, at least compared to white glue. It will glue most substances in a manner of seconds, including your fingers. It will actually glue fingers together much better than it will many of the things you're trying to fix. Super glue is not much different than the two-part epoxy previously described, which uses a chemical reaction to form a permanent adhesive. You mix the two parts together, wait a few minutes, and a permanent bond is created.

The number-one ingredient in super glue is cyanoacrylate, which is an acrylic resin. All cyanoacrylate needs to harden is water, and almost every surface has microscopic droplets of water on it that helps speed the process along. Wiping the broken piece with a damp rag will make the process even faster, but adding more super glue will slow it down, because more water is needed to use all of the cyanoacrylate molecules. Come to think of it, using super glue in the Sahara may not work so well. Anyway, after wiping down the broken piece, just put a little glue on the broken piece and hold together for five seconds to get a fast, permanent bond.

> ## Brain Fart
>
> There are three kinds of scientists: those who can count and those who can't.

Fingers are the perfect gluing surface for super glue. They are rough and have plenty of places to create strong bonds. Also, your body is full of water, so the cyanoacrylate can sink in and harden. Faster than you can say "#$&*#@," your fingers are glued. Nail polish remover will help to dissolve the bonds.

Super glue is even finding its way into the hospital to close wounds. Normal super glue contains a chemical that kills skin cells, but medical super glue replaces that chemical. If they ever sell that over the counter, we will be able to take care of our own power toy (oops . . . power tool) accidents.

HOW DO PORTABLE NAIL GUNS WORK?

Nail guns come in two basic varieties: compressor driven and fuel-cell driven. They both accomplish the same task, but the fuel-cell types have a few advantages. Cordless nail guns are relatively quiet, except when they fire. Compressors are noisy. I'm talking front-row-heavy-metal-concert noisy. And the compressor nail gun is also connected by an air hose for you to trip over. Cordless nail guns give you the freedom to roam.

Cordless nail guns use a fuel cell, most often filled with liquefied petroleum gas, and a spark plug powered by an internal battery. An internal piston, similar to the ones in your car engine, pushes the nail into the wood when the nail gun safety and trigger are depressed simultaneously. The fuel cells can get expensive, but that is the cost of freedom.

The nail gun fuel cells are also different than the fuel-cell technology that is always mentioned as the future of auto-mobiles. Nail gun fuel cells are just containers of fuel, but car fuel-cells are devices that deliver electricity from hydrogen and oxygen. This process is just a reverse of one of your high school chemistry experiments. Passing electricity through water causes hydrogen and oxygen to be released. Car fuel cells just do the opposite.

Owning a portable nail gun will cause you to attempt home-improvement projects you never would have tackled before. Crown molding used to be for experts, but with a nail gun and a compound miter saw you can look like a pro. But remember: Nail guns are dangerous. A safety trigger must be depressed along with the trigger to fire the nail. It is possible to depress the safety with your foot and nail your foot to the floor. OUCH.

HOW DO PLASMA CUTTERS CUT?

Plasma cutters cut through metal like a knife through butter. For a long time, plasma cutters were only found in professional machine shops. The prices have now dropped to where they are affordable for the weekend metal worker. The name *plasma cutter* also sounds really cool, like something out of *Star Wars*. Sorry I couldn't take your call, I was out in the shop using my plasma cutter.

Obviously, plasma cutters use plasma to cut with, but how? And what the heck is plasma anyway? Let's review. Plasma is the fourth state of matter, after solid, liquid, and gas. Plasma is an extremely excited gas, usually created by very high temperatures. At these high temps, some electrons are stripped from the outside of the gas ions and the gas conducts electricity. Plasma already has a big impact in our life, we just don't know it. The sun, fluorescent lights, neon lights, and lightning are all plasma.

Brain Fart

If metal-skinned aliens invade Earth, plasma cutters will make great weapons.

Now that we know what plasma is, how does it cut metal? The cutter uses a high-speed jet of plasma to melt through the metal. The jet is focused to cut a very small line in the metal. At the heart of the cutter is a negatively charged electrode. A compressed gas is passed by the electrode toward the metal surface and becomes ionized when the electrode is switched on. The plasma conducts the electric arc (a mini lightning bolt) to the metal piece allowing you to slice right through it. The fast-moving plasma also carries away the melted metal and most of the heat, leaving you with a very clean cut.

Plasma cutters only work on materials that conduct electricity, so wood and plastic are out. But they are a great way to cut most metals.

HOW DO CFLS WORK?

Unless you live in an unlit cave, you probably already know that *CFL* stands for compact fluorescent light. The small spiral bulbs are gradually replacing the incandescent bulb that ruled the lighting world for the last century. CFLs were developed in response to the oil crisis of the early seventies but were shelved when oil got cheap again. The bulbs are expensive, but the price has dropped like a rock over the last ten years.

Fluorescent lights work by passing a large electric current through a gas and creating plasma. The gas is a mixture of argon, neon, and/or krypton, with a few drops of mercury. The large current causes electrons of the mercury atoms to jump to a higher level as they absorb energy. As the electrons jump back down to a lower level, they each emit a photon of light. The emitted photon is ultraviolet (UV), which we can't see. The UV photon strikes a coating on the inside of the glass called a phosphor. The phosphor glows and produces the visible light. This process happens without using heat like an incandescent bulb, so CFLs use less energy and are better for the environment.

The CFL base contains the electronics needed to excite the gas. The base contains a small circuit board with rectifiers, a capacitor, and two switching transistors connected together designed to create a high-frequency current. The resulting high frequency, around 40 kHz or higher, is applied to the bulb tube.

CFLs still take a minute or so to warm up to their full brightness, but we can get used to that. We have to. CFLs are going to be a part of our lives from now on. Also, these bulbs last longer due to their lack of metal filament, which means that we have to change them a lot less often. Thank you science for both saving the environment and making less work for guys!

HOW DO GUN SILENCERS WORK?

Professional hitmen have used them for years in their quest for the kill, and many of us normal people use them in our video games. The sound from a gunshot is created by the exploding powder as it ignites to fire the bullet. Sound waves are vibrations transmitted through a medium, such as air, and the speed at which the wave travels depends on the properties of the medium (temperature and pressure when talking about air). There is a tremendous amount of air vibration that comes with the explosion of a gun firing, and if you can reduce one of the properties of the medium (temperature and pressure), you can reduce the sound wave.

Silencers work similarly to the muffler on your car. They both increase the volume at the end of a barrel. The exhaust gas now has a place to expand and cool before it finally leaves the silencer. As the gas expands, the pressure drops, and with the dropped pressure comes reduced noise. The silencer also contains baffles—small metal plates inside the silencer that help dissipate the sound energy. The bullet leaves with a little pfft instead of a large bang. Most silencers also slow down the bullet to subsonic speeds so there isn't a little sonic boom.

WHY DOES A WHIP CRACK?

Indiana Jones has saved many lives with the crack of a whip. And many of us popped our teammates on the ass with a towel using the same principle. But why does a whip crack?

The whip (or towel) cracks because the speed of the end actually exceeds the speed of sound. You get a mini sonic boom as the towel end lands on an unsuspecting butt. A sound wave is created any time you move something. If you move slower than the speed of sound (about 760 miles per hour or 340 meters per second), the center of the wave keeps moving and you get circular waves that are off-centered. If you exceed the speed of sound, the waves will trail the source of the sound. This causes the wavefronts to line up. If you get a bunch of wavefronts lined up, you get a higher pressure wave. Higher pressure creates a sonic boom. Anything that exeeds the speed of sound will create a sonic boom, including jet fighters and rifle bullets.

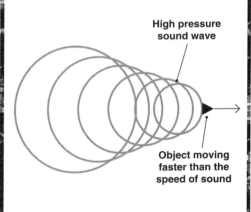

Creation of a Sonic Boom

High pressure
sound wave

Object moving
faster than the
speed of sound

EIGHT: THE CALL OF THE WILD

Animals bring us tons of enjoyment and many laughs. Companionship and a sympathetic ear are all great reasons for having a pet. Your dog never tells you to stop whining when you rant about a bad call during a game. Your cat just sits and purrs as you lament a lost job or lost love. We love going to the zoo, so our love of animals extends well beyond just pets. Even the largest theme park in the world is designed around a rodent. Over half of all our sports teams are named after members of the animal kingdom.

We also fear certain animals. Bears, alligators, and snakes are great for our sports teams, but we really don't want to see one in our back-yard. All guys are allowed one irrational fear of animals. You are free to hate spiders, snakes, cockroaches, or even vicious attacking rabbits with long, sharp teeth.

In this chapter we'll examine our love for animals and a few animal myths. Can you outrun a gator? Why do coyotes howl? Why is man's best friend a dog? Why do we get a dog as a best friend but women get diamonds? Why do men inherently mistrust cats? Do bulls really hate red?

In addition to animals, we love all parts of nature. We gaze at a beautiful sunset with the one we love. As we stare, we wonder why the sky appears red at dusk but University-of-North-Carolina-blue during the day? We love diamonds, gold, and silver. What makes stones precious? What makes light sweet crude oil so expensive? Inquiring minds want to know! So grab your leash and let's examine the world of animals and nature!

WHY DO MOST MEN LOVE DOGS?

Dogs long ago earned the moniker of man's best friend; it is a badge of honor for most pooches. Your dog greets you at the door and licks your face, regardless of what mood you come home in. Your dog is the perfect conversation starter on a Saturday trip to the park. Almost no woman can pass by a cute dog without saying something. Your dog will also bark to wake you during a fire or burglary.

Loyal, friendly, forgiving, great listeners, and icebreakers with potential dates—dogs enjoy the company of man. If you scold a dog, it will sulk into the corner only to beg forgiveness a few minutes later. Dogs don't need flowers, chocolate, or an expensive dinner to forgive you when you take a bad day out on them.

Of course, like in any relationship, dogs often make you mad. They occasionally leave little dog bombs of recycled food in your house and occasionally want to hump the leg of a houseguest. Dog humping is really funny if it happens to an annoying relative, but it's not so funny if it happens to your rich, old Aunt Jewel. She might just cut you and the dog out of the will. It's also definitely not funny if a "special friend" is paying the first visit to your house.

Dogs are man's best friend because of their loyalty—a trait that ranks number one on most men's lists of desirable traits. We like our human friends to be loyal, especially if we try to date their sister (or their brother). We like our sports stars loyal. We hear them say "It's not about the money," and then we get angry when they sign a huge contract and leave our

> ## Brain Fart
>
> Dogs are wonderful, but occasionally they want to make love to the leg of a houseguest. They don't ask and they won't bring flowers.

favorite team. And most of all, we like our pets loyal. Dogs win the all-time loyalty award. They stick by us no matter what!

The science of why we love man's best friend is interesting. Our brains have neat little chemicals called endorphins. Endorphins are a type of hormone that reduces pain and produces a calmness that makes us feel good. This hormone actually acts in much the same manner as morphine, and it is completely legal. Endorphins cause the great feeling we get after a run or an intense workout, but more subtle things can also cause this reaction. A good laugh and getting outside are two subtle ways to increase your endorphins. Dogs force us to walk them whether we want to or not. And of course, we always get a good laugh when the dog lets one rip. Dogs help us smile, and smiles lead to endorphins. Don't you just love science!

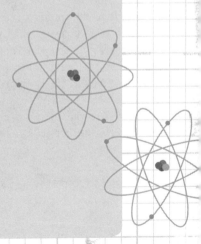

WHY ARE DOG FARTS SILENT?

Dogs bring new meaning to the term *SBD* (silent but deadly). They pass gas, walk to the other side of the room, and leave us to gasp in terror from the smell. Dogs create gas in their bodies the same way us humans do: by what they eat and how much air they gulp down. But why are dog farts mostly silent? Here is my theory on dog farts, backed up with explanations. Feel free to research this topic if you need a dissertation topic.

First, dogs don't have butt cheeks. Since they don't have butt cheeks, they don't have much to vibrate as the offending gas leaves. All sound is created by vibrations. Without butt cheeks, the gas just escapes the opening with a minimum of vibrations created in the air. This would be like playing a clarinet without the reed. You could still get air through it, but it wouldn't create much sound.

Second, dog sphincters are looser than human sphincters. This is similar to the balloon-neck trick we used to annoy our third-grade teacher. If you stretch the neck tight as the balloon empties, you get a high-pitched shriek. But if you just let the balloon go, it will fly off in a mostly silent rush of air. Of course, this leads to the question: Why doesn't my dog fly across the room after letting one rip? I think that has to do with the weight of the dog. Maybe little furballs do take off after a particularly gassy exchange. Of course, a few dogs do make noise as they pass gas, but most just sneak one in and leave us gasping.

WHY DO COYOTES HOWL?

The long howl of a coyote is a staple of country life, but why does a coyote howl? Coyotes howl to announce their territory. A long howl is followed by silence so neighboring coyotes can announce their space. Coyotes are very territorial, but also very respectful. They tend to leave neighboring coyotes alone and hunt away from their direction. They also howl to call their family home after a day of hunting. A coyote family will occasionally all howl together to announce their presence and number. And I imagine that lonely coyotes howl for a little companionship.

Coyotes live in small family packs composed of a male, female, and any offspring that haven't left home yet. Sometimes, if the alpha male and female agree, they will adopt a strange coyote. They will coordinate attacks on large prey, but they usually only attack small animals so coordinated attacks are rare.

CAN YOU OUTRUN AN ALLIGATOR?

We've all heard the numbers. Alligators can run 30, 40, or even 50 miles per hour, and you should run in a zigzag pattern to outrun them. These are both great exaggerations. I think we should call these suburban myths, myths that live on in the suburbs due to kids preying on the fears of other kids. I first heard these numbers when I was in elementary school. Little Ricky first told me, and he sure sounded convincing. As a slow kid growing up in Florida, I was scared. Common sense will tell you that any animal that big with tiny legs (25 cm) is going to struggle as a sprinter, but that didn't help me in the fourth grade.

It appears that no credible research group has ever measured the speed of an alligator, but you have to love the Australians. They have measured the speed of Australian freshwater crocodiles, and for me that is close enough. Australian freshwater crocodiles top out at a whopping 11 miles per hour. That's faster than I jog but slower than I run while being chased by a twelve-foot reptile with giant teeth.

> **Did You Know?**
>
> Most experts agree that the cheetah is the fastest land animal, clocking out between 60 and 70 miles per hour. Possibly even more amazing is the Indo-Pacific Sailfish that has topped 65 miles per hour in the water.

The science of outrunning gators comes down to speed versus acceleration. Gators are extremely strong animals that rely on their strength to survive. They are lurkers who lay hidden in the water and wait for unsuspecting prey to wander by. But don't worry, if you see a gator, you can outrun it.

Gators are not fast, but they are quick. They rely on the element of surprise to capture food. They can lunge one body length in a blur of jaws and teeth. Over that one body length, they have incredible acceleration. They can reach full speed in one twenty-five-centimeter-leg-driven step. However, they slow down as fast as they started. If you can avoid that lunge, you are safe and the gator will go hungry. Running in a zigzag pattern will give your friends a good laugh, but it won't necessarily help you. And trust me, if a gator makes a surprise lunge at you, your brain won't think about zigzagging.

Even so, it is probably a good idea not to walk right by the edge of a gator-infested river. And definitely don't limp right by the edge of a gator-infested river. Gators tend to feast on already dead carcasses and injured or weak animals, so if you are aware and in relatively good shape, avoiding being gator food is easy.

You can also try to avoid alligators altogether by living in the suburbs. There aren't many gator-infested rivers in suburbia, just an occasional gator-infested pool in your neighbor's yard. If you live in the burbs, make sure your children keep the myth alive. You can also live in a major city and you will be completely safe, as long as you avoid that alligator living in the sewer.

WILL COCKROACHES SURVIVE A NUCLEAR BLAST?

Cockroaches are resilient. You spray them with bug spray, and many just laugh at you as they scurry off. You step on them, and they manage to find the tread of your shoe and limp off to have more babies to infest your house. They sure are hard to get rid of. Of course, a nuclear bomb would get rid of them. Or would it?

Any roaches close to ground zero would be vaporized, so they don't always survive nuclear blasts. But cockroaches farther away from ground zero may have a better chance. They may actually have a better chance than us people.

To understand why, we have to look at radiation tolerance. A rem is a measured dose of radiation that causes a measured amount of human tissue damage. A dose of 800 rems or more is considered lethal for humans. Our friend the American cockroach can withstand up to about 67,500 rems before it dies. German cockroaches are even tougher; they can survive over 100,000 rems. Cockroaches can also bury themselves in the dirt for months at a time, which can help them avoid fallout.

Cockroaches are tough. The flip side of that is humans are wimpy. Only 800 rems and we are toast. We need to get tougher as a species. Maybe we should forgo the lead sheet at our next dental X-ray to help toughen us up. Maybe our dentist could X-ray each tooth individually. A single X-ray is only in the neighborhood of one-tenth of a rem, so you would need plenty. It might be easier to just get rid of all nuclear weapons,

> **Did You Know?**
> A cockroach can live over a week without its head before it starves to death.

which gets my vote. Cockroaches and people would both be safer.

In my own scientific research, I have discovered that smooth-soled dress shoes are more deadly than nuclear bombs. My dress shoes have killed more cockroaches than I can count. Sneakers give the roaches a chance. Each roach that limps away can produce up to 400 eggs in its lifetime. That doesn't sound bad until you imagine 400 roaches in your kitchen at the same time. And also, all 400 babies can each have 400 more.

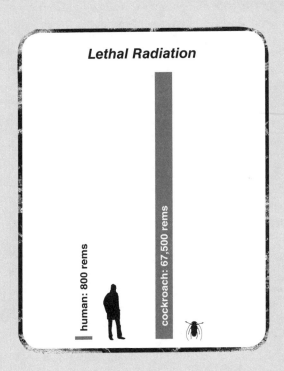

Lethal Radiation

human: 800 rems

cockroach: 67,500 rems

WHY DO MEN DISTRUST CATS?

Men fall into two distinct categories: cat lovers and cat haters. No middle ground here. You either love them or you hate them. I think this stems psychologically from our childhood. If you had cats in your house before the age of ten, you will most likely be a cat lover. No cat in the house as a child and you will be a hater. The science of memories is really quite amazing. Episodic memories are related to single episodes. These memories are a collection of what happened as we aged. We not only store the actual memory but also any pleasant associations. If we had a cat in the house as a kid, we usually have great episodic memories that contained the cat. If your first encounter with a cat was your girlfriend's cat peeing on your letter jacket, the episodic memory will not be good.

What about people who just hate (or love) cats and never had one growing up? That's due to semantic memory. Semantic memory is concept based and unrelated to any specific experience, which means you make a value judgment (cats are inherently evil/good) without any experience to back it up.

Cats and dogs are portrayed as mortal enemies. So if a dog is a man's best friend, then by natural extension that means men are going to distrust cats. Cats and dogs have peacefully coexisted in many houses, but the cat is always in charge. Cats can also be loyal, but it has to be their idea. Cats can also be trained not to leave stinky piles of recycled food around the house, and if they do the dog will clean it up. There's one benefit of having cats and dogs both in your house: You won't have to clean the litter box as often. Talk about the ultimate recycling setup.

Cats are the antithesis of dogs. Where a dog will spend three hours playing Frisbee with you, a cat would rather take a nap. Dogs greet you after a hard day. Cats might, if they haven't had a hard day. How does a housecat ever have a bad day? Alley cats have to fight for life and food, but a housecat gets three squares and tons of places to sleep. Dogs bring you the newspaper; cats bring you dead rodents.

If you ever watched Walt Disney movies as a child, you will also develop a distrust of cats. This distrust is related to what we learned over the years. If we continuously see cats portrayed as evil, we eventually assume all cats are evil. In most Disney movies, cats are portrayed as sinister creatures. They sneak around always getting man's best friend in trouble. The classic anticat movie is *The Lady and the Tramp*, but many others show the same sneaky, troublemaking side of cats. Walt Disney truly hated cats. Of course, Walt's empire is built around a mouse, so his hatred of cats is natural. I wonder if he was born that way or if he had negative experiences with cats growing up?

Did You Know?

Cat urine glows under ultraviolet light.

I love cats and they elevate my endorphins, but I have good cats. If you have an evil, sinister, Disney-esque cat, you won't have an endorphin release. If your cat is a loner, maybe you should try putting your cat on a leash and taking it out in the sunshine for a walk. Both the walk and the sunshine will help your endorphin levels.

WHY DO GREAT WHITE SHARKS SWIM FOR THEIR LIVES?

Great white sharks are the most awesome predators in the sea; they are the quintessential killing machine. Like all fish, great white sharks have gills that pull oxygen out of the seawater so they can breathe. Great whites use a process called ram ventilation to move the water over their gills. That means they must keep swimming to keep the water moving. They even swim when they are asleep! Their brain shuts down while they keep moving, similar to sleepwalking. This is also a defense mechanism we develop for long-winded meetings at work.

Most species of sharks have the ability to pull water past their gills as they sit still. This method of breathing is called buccal pumping. The cheek muscles contract and pull seawater over the gills as they sit still. Great whites, makos, whale sharks, and a few other species have lost this ability over the years and must swim to live.

DO SHARKS REALLY HAVE TWO PENISES?

A trip to the aquarium is great fun for the family, but it can lead to some embarrassing questions if you go with kids. The tunnel through the shark tank is often the scene of my favorite "what-is-that?" moment. Most male sharks have two long appendages hanging out their underside near the rear. These gigantic appendages are called claspers—an easier word to use with kids—and in reality these function like a shark penis. Male sharks are real proud.

Why two? Shark experts think it allows them to mate on either side. Swimming and having sex can't be easy, so two penises increase the chances. Most of the time only one clasper is in use, but there have been a few reports of some sharks using both at the same time. What a lucky lady!

Brain Fart

Sharks don't have arms, so male sharks will bite to hold on to their lady friends. Next time you see a shark with scars, realize it could have been from a night of romance.

DO BULLS REALLY HATE RED?

No, bulls are actually colorblind. Bullfighters still use red capes because of tradition. The color red probably symbolizes blood. By the way, the bullfight never ends up good for the bull. You give up an afternoon to watch the bullfights; the bull, unfortunately, gives up a little more.

The human eye contains two separate receptors: rods and cones. Rods determine the intensity of light in black and white. Cones allow us to see colors. Cows' eyes don't contain cones. The ability to perceive color actually takes a much larger brain than the bull has. Our brain is large enough to see color: The bull's is not. Bull's brains are large enough to see female cows, though. And the bulls keep the herd growing so us big-brained people can turn them into T-bones and leather couches.

The fact is that many animals see exclusively in black and white. Some animals have limited color blindness. A human eye contains three different receptors for the three colors of light: red, green, and blue. If a particular animal species is missing one or more receptor, the animal is colorblind. Dogs and cats are thought to be able to see some color but not the entire spectrum. They also have more rods to help with their night vision. Daytime birds have a full range of color vision. That is why male birds are so brightly colored—to attract the ladies. Owls have virtually no color vision.

> ### Did You Know?
> Ernest Hemingway first popularized running with the bulls in Pamplona, and it is just crazy enough to be shown on CNN every year, so more people want to do it. The people from Pamplona love it because they get a chance for more gore— most of which comes from tourists.

Whether you are a matador or someone running with the bulls in Pamplona, it's movement and teasing that bulls hate. If you stand in front of a bull and wave a green tablecloth at him long enough, he'll get pissed and charge. If he gets mad and you keep teasing, he'll charge again.

HOW DOES BEING WHITE HELP A POLAR BEAR?

The white color of a polar bear helps it stay nearly invisible on the frozen ice where it hunts. A polar bear's skin is actually black; you can see this by looking at its nose and lips. A polar bear has two layers of fur: a dense undercoat to insulate its body and a layer of longer, translucent, hollow hairs. The hollow hairs help to insulate its body just like a double-paned window helps insulate your house. The bear appears white because all of this fur reflects the white sunlight and the light bouncing off of the ice. Due to its built-in camouflage, the world's largest land predator is free to hide until dinner swims by.

Brain Fart

A day without sunshine is like night.

WHY IS THE SKY BLUE?

Technically the sky isn't blue. It only appears blue during the midday sun. At other times it appears red, orange, and even black. Light from the sun is actually white, but white is a mixture of all the different colors. As the photons of light move through the atmosphere, they strike all of the stuff present in the atmosphere, which is composed primarily of nitrogen, oxygen, water vapor, and a few other trace gases. The atmosphere also contains solid particles like dust and smoke. What happens when the photons strike depends on the size of the particles they hit. If they hit a large dust particle, the particle will reflect most of the colors and appear whitish in color, like clouds. Volcanic dust and smog can also lead to slightly different shades of white (or gray if you live in a big city).

> **Did You Know?**
>
> To see a rainbow you must have your back to the sun.

As the light hits smaller gas molecules, some is absorbed, some passes right through, and some is scattered. The longer-wavelength red, orange, and yellow tend to pass right through, so when you look directly at the sun it appears a yellowish color. The blue light tends to be scattered the most because it has a short wavelength. This scattered light reaches our eye from the rest of the sky. The sky appears blue!

When the sun is low on the horizon (at dusk and dawn), the light has to take a longer trip through the atmosphere. The longer trip allows more blue light to be scattered before it reaches us. Since more blue light is scattered to others on the globe, only the longer reds and oranges reach our eye. We get a beautiful sunrise or sunset, perfect for a romantic moment with a special person.

At night the sky appears black. Remember: If you don't have white light, you don't have color.

WHAT CAN PETROLEUM DO FOR US?

Since the 1950s, petroleum has been the major form of energy for the world. Petroleum goes beyond making gas, kerosene, fuel oil, and the fuel compounds. It is also important in making many other products, such as plastics, wax, petroleum jelly, fertilizers, and asphalt. Although we are going to run out in our lifetime, we still crave the simple fuel.

Petroleum, also called crude oil, was formed over millions of years after dead sea life settled on the bottom of the ocean. Heat and pressure transformed the dead matter into the oil we love. Crude oil out of the ground can run from black and thick all the way to greenish yellow and thin. Low-density oil is called light and delivers higher amounts of gasoline, kerosene, and fuel oil. Sweet petroleum is crude oil with a minimum of sulfur contamination. Light sweet crude oil is the most desirable and the most expensive per barrel. Heavy sour crude oil is less expensive to buy but costs more to refine.

Did You Know?

Natural gas (from the actual gas company) has no odor. The smell is added artificially so leaks can be detected.

WHY ARE DIAMONDS SO HARD?

Carbon bonds in tons of cool ways. Graphite (pencil lead) is a boring but useful type of carbon. And carbon is present in almost every fuel source we use. Diamonds—an allotropic form of carbon—are a transparent crystal desired for two main characteristics: hardness and the ability to refract light.

The hardest known natural substance, diamonds are useful in industry and jewelry making. Jewel-quality diamonds are extremely durable and can only be scratched by other diamonds. This isn't very smart since it will damage both diamonds, but you can try it if you don't believe me. The hardness allows them to put up with the stress of day-to-day life. They will maintain their luster and shine regardless of how many times you bang it into something. Diamonds do cut glass, but so do many other minerals, like quartz.

Quartz won't cut granite though. Industrial diamonds are impregnated into saw blades and used to cut and polish all manner of stone. You can buy diamond-coated saw blades at your local home-improvement store. Buying a saw blade for an engagement present is usually frowned upon, but you can try. You could even mount it on a big gold chain to increase the tacky factor.

So why are diamonds so hard? Although graphite is pure carbon, the graphite crystals are bonded by sharing electrons (called a covalent bond) in flat layers. Covalent bonds are very strong. The attraction between adjacent flat layers is not very strong, so a layer rubs off easily as you write with a pencil. Diamond crystallizes in a three-dimensional hexagonal pattern, but the distance between adjacent layers is much closer, which means that the bonds are equally strong in all directions and don't rub off. You can break a diamond along a flat cleavage plane, but it is difficult. It takes a very hard blow from a trained gemologist.

The ability to refract light is another great reason the diamond is coveted. Refraction is the bending of light waves as they enter a new substance. The light bends because it slows down. It is like riding a tricycle as a kid. If one wheel goes off the road into the sand, you will be automatically turned in that direction. Since diamonds slow down light more than almost any other substance, they bend light more. Diamonds are also broken to form many facets because each facet can catch light and bend it toward another facet to escape. This causes the diamond to sparkle as it is moved around.

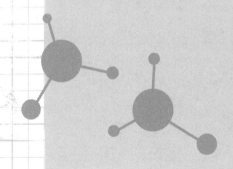

Did You Know?

Diamonds won't dissolve in acid.

Diamond engagement rings are a relatively new but very smart advertising gimmick. Ads have led us to give diamonds as a token of our love. We not only give little ones, but we spend two or three months of our salary on bigger ones. Season tickets to your favorite sports team are also a token of love, but they just don't carry the same weight.

NINE: THE FAIRER SEX

Finally a chapter containing information about women from a guy's perspective! Nothing excites and confuses men more than women. This chapter will attempt to explain the science of the female body, mind, and soul. PMS, women's intuition, the extra rib, and more scary womanly things will be covered. You may know how a fuel injector works, but women will always be a mystery to most men.

We won't always admit it, but we spend many hours wondering how women work. We admire women. We question other guys about women. We even occasionally ask women themselves, but we still don't understand them. However, in my years of studying women, I have come to a few scientific "truths" that I will share with you.

You must not let women know about the existence of the following few pages. Read them, but move the bookmark when you are done. You know that she will peek at this book to see what you are reading if it's left out. (Have you ever peeked in a woman's book to see what she was reading? I didn't think so.) Only men will understand these truths I'm about to share. You are allowed to discuss the ideas with other men but not with your better half under any circumstances. So turn off that chick flick as we examine the world of women.

WHAT IS WOMEN'S INTUITION?

Intuition is defined as being able to perceive something without conscious reasoning. Women's intuition has been around since the dawn of time. Think your mother had eyes in the back of her head? Nope, it was her woman's intuition. All guys understand Spidey Sense and we are okay with it. Women's intuition is just Spidey Sense without the spider bite. Maybe Peter Parker was just in touch with his feminine side. It works for him. At last count it has saved his life over a thousand times.

Men have been taught cause and effect for years in science classes, sports, and life. If we do something, it will cause something else to happen. If we miss an open shot in a basketball game, we may not get the ball again. Cause and effect doesn't allow most of us to act on a gut feeling. We want proof. Guys just need to reread all of the *Spider-Man* comics and watch the movies to get better in tune with our intuition.

> **Did You Know?**
>
> In the original *Spider-Man* comic book, a radioactive spider bit Peter Parker. In the movie version, a genetically engineered spider bit him.

Many experts claim that women's intuition is due to the fact that women are better at reading nonverbal communication, and this may be true. Women can ferret out exactly what is meant by the slightest smile or gesture, while men are simple breeds who only notice things when we are knocked over the head. Although a British study found men were just as adept at picking out fake smiles as women, men still struggle with acting on that fact. Pretty people could lie to us all day and we would gladly believe them.

Men have always been encouraged to make logical conclusions. We have been trained to act logically by parents, teachers, and coaches our whole life. Logical means we have to think and act rationally. We are taught everything follows a set progression. The problem is that relationships aren't always rational. We need to learn to be irrational by developing our intuition.

Some experts think that women's intuition works because women are more in tune with their feelings. From almost day one, girls have been encouraged to act on their feelings. They are allowed to say "women's intuition" and get an immediate out. Meanwhile, men were taught to hide their feelings and be tough. Those lines are starting to be blurred nowadays, but they are still there. Whatever the reason, most women have it and most men don't.

Scientifically Speaking

Intuition comes very close to clairvoyance; it appears to be the extrasensory perception of reality.

—Alexis Carrel

WHAT IS PMS?

PMS stands for premenstrual syndrome, which leads me to wonder why it's not PS. Maybe PS was already spoken for by the letter-writing crowd. Many men would probably say PMS should be a four-letter word. PMS is real and affects women to a variety of different degrees. It is a collection of up to 150 symptoms that may all appear at the same time. Depression, mood swings, headaches, fatigue, and insomnia are just a few of the symptoms. PMS starts about two weeks prior to the start of menstruation and tapers off as menstruation is reached. Medical experts think it's due to changing hormone levels, but the truth is they don't know. The numbers vary from different sources, but 60 to 85 percent of all women who are menstruating experience some form of PMS. The level can vary from "I'm cramping" to "Drop the remote or you die!" Some doctors even say it is a socially constructed disease and not a real malady. I feel confident that all of those doctors are male and clueless.

I am one of the lucky ones; my partner has never made me give up the remote. But growing up with a mom and a sister, I can give some advice for dealing with PMS: Kill it with kindness. When PMS is camped at your doorstep, you don't want to debate paint color, movie choices, or come home late. The most important thing to remember about PMS is she's right and you're wrong. The words "Yes, dear" have also been known to be effective.

DO WOMEN HAVE EXTRA RIBS?

A long-standing myth is that women have one extra rib. Most normal skeletons—male or female—have twelve sets of ribs, no more, no less. The extra rib story comes from the Bible, which states the Creator removed a rib from Adam so he could have a partner. I am confident Adam was glad to have a woman around, but I wonder if he would have willingly given up a rib. Maybe Adam started out with a cervical rib, or maybe he only had eleven after surgery. Either way, most normal skeletons have twelve now.

There is a rare genetic disorder that can cause people to be born with an extra rib, called a cervical rib. This extra rib grows out of the lowest cervical (neck) vertebra. It is usually found only on one side and affects less than 0.5 percent of the population. This extra rib can lead to neck, arm, and shoulder pain since it presses on the nerves on that side of the body. In a few rarer cases, people actually have one on both sides.

Did You Know?

Babies are actually born with kneecaps but they won't show up on an X-ray. The patella in babies is actually cartilage and doesn't start to ossify (turn into a bone) until the child is three to five years of age. This makes sense since most of a baby's bones will continue to develop over the first few years of life.

CAN MALES GET PREGNANT?

In the human world, no. But in the seahorse world, men are the ones who get pregnant. Seahorses are one of the most curious of all fish because they have a horse head, a monkey tail, and the males get pregnant.

As with most species of animals, the male shows off to attract a mate. Once a suitable mate is found, the male starts the "dance of love." The couple then intertwines their tails and begins a long, slow courtship. After up to eight hours of cuddling, the female deposits her eggs into the lucky guy. Male seahorses have a pouch that can contain all of the baby seahorses as they grow. During this time, the male moves very little and loses all of his color. Eventually the male undergoes a painful looking birth as he releases approximately two hundred baby "fry" into the water. Dad never gives them any help after that, but neither does the mom. Only a few of these babies reach adulthood to repeat the dance of love.

> **Did You Know?**
>
> An elephant's pregnancy lasts twenty-two months. Probably not the science fact to mention to your partner if she complains about being pregnant.

There is a recent case of a transgender female to male who became the first human guy to get pregnant. Although pregnancy was possible for him (her), it isn't possible for biologically born males.

DOES BRAINWASHING WORK?

Brainwashing is called thought reform. Although it probably doesn't occur on the level that some Hollywood movies show, it will still work. Cult members, kids, and POWs are the most common groups this is tried on, but you can even do it to yourself. Try saying "I love my job" twenty-five times every hour. Your spirits will lift about your job—that is if you can stop laughing long enough to think about it. Try saying "My partner is incredibly good looking" all the time, and he/she will begin to look hotter.

Your mother probably brainwashed you as a kid. She convinced you to do things you wouldn't otherwise do, and you went along with it until you were a teen. Suddenly, as an adult, you horrify yourself by repeating one of your mom's pet sayings. See! Motherly brainwashing at its best.

Most serious attempts at brainwashing rely on isolation and guilt. The brainwashers isolate people and break them down. The victims may eventually conform to the brainwasher's thoughts. Maybe you've heard of the Stockholm syndrome, named after an incident involving a bank robbery in Stockholm. After six days, the hostages actually defended the robbers as the police ended the siege. It is also called trauma-bonding. Hostage victims will empathize with their captors and even bond with them. In a few cases, the hostages eventually did things they never would have before.

Does brainwashing work? Just say the following two thousand times in the next day—brainwashing works, brainwashing works, brainwashing works . . .

WHY IS IT OKAY TO HATE SOME FEMALES?

Guys love most females, but they definitely don't like female mosquitoes. Both male and female mosquitoes live off sugar from plant nectars and fruits, but only female mosquitoes bite since they need protein and iron from blood to produce eggs. One blood meal is needed for each 250-egg nest the female lays. Females can live from up to a week to several weeks depending on whether they get slapped (or zapped). Males generally only live four or five days and die after mating.

When mosquitoes bite, they inject a little of their saliva to help them suck your blood. The saliva keeps their proboscis (long sucker thing) from coagulating as they gorge themselves on your blood. It is this transfer of saliva that leads to the spread of diseases like malaria, West Nile virus, and encephalitis. After they pull out and fly off (or you violently squash them), a tiny bit of saliva is left in the wound. Your body responds to the saliva by making the area red, inflamed, and itchy.

Did You Know?

Window screens and television have been credited with lowering mosquito-borne diseases. One keeps us in at night and the other keeps the bugs out at night.

HOW DO TATTOOS WORK?

Tattoos are no longer only for sailors, NBA players, and bikers. Over the past ten years or so the tattoo business has exploded into the mainstream. From simple butterflies to elaborate fire-breathing dragons, tattoos have proliferated—and more and more women are making the decision to get tattooed. Maybe the cute, conservative woman in the cubicle next to you has a secret tat she doesn't let you know about. Tats show an inner rebellious side that most men secretly crave. You see a tat and you know she has a wild side.

The secret to the tat is the tat gun. The gun is essentially a handheld sewing machine. The tiny needle penetrates your skin between 50 and 3,000 times a minute and leaves a drop of ink each time. The ink is only deposited about 1 millimeter into your skin. Skin consists of two main layers: epidermis and dermis. The epidermis is the outer four or five layers that are continually peeling off. The dermis layer is deeper and more stable. The ink is injected into this base layer and will stay there for years with only minor fading.

The artist starts by tracing a stencil onto your body. Next a very thin outline is done in black ink. The artist then adds colors and shades the artwork to turn you into a living canvas. Good tattoo artists are just that, artists. Their work is fabulous. They can create any artwork you desire, only this art lasts forever. In your house you can trash a picture and replace it. Trashing a tattoo is difficult and expensive. We'll get to that in a minute.

As we age, our skin droops, stretches, and sags. We hope that it never will, but gravity will take its toll on your body. A cute butterfly is hot when a woman is twenty, but what about when she's seventy? Butterflies begin to look like pterodactyls. Chinese letters turn into road maps of London. Tribal tats begin to look like Salvador Dali paintings. And tattooing a loved one's name seemed like a good idea at the time, until they are unloved. Of course, you can always cover the name with a tribal tat or opt for a more painful solution.

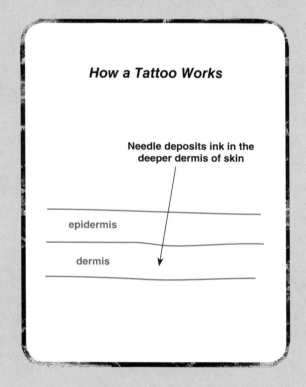

How a Tattoo Works

Needle deposits ink in the deeper dermis of skin

epidermis

dermis

HOW DO YOU GET RID OF A TATTOO?

Someday a woman may have to explain that tattoo to her five-year-old, or have to go to long lengths to hide that pterodactyl from her boss. Will she regret it then? Or maybe you will have to wear long sleeves to hide that ring of barbed wire around your shrinking bicep. One option is to have it removed. Tattoo removal is expensive, painful, and time consuming.

The major way to remove a tattoo is with a laser. Tiny pulses of laser energy penetrate into the dermis and break up the tattoo pigment. Your body's own immune system then carries away the remaining little pieces over the next few weeks. The number of treatments depends on the size, complexity, and color of your tat, and you may be left with a blemish even after the treatments.

Black ink is the easiest to remove because black pigment absorbs all colors of laser lights. Most individual colors only have certain wave-lengths that they absorb, and the laser's wavelength needs to be adjusted for different colors. Yellows and greens are much harder to remove. It is much more expensive to remove a tattoo than it is to get one, but it may be worth it to get rid of that pterodactyl. A green pterodactyl may just stay with you forever.

> **Did You Know?**
>
> Tigers actually have their own form of tattoos. They have striped skin in addition to striped fur.

HOW DOES HAIR COLOR WORK?

It is estimated that almost 75 percent of all women color their hair, but the number of men coloring their hair is rapidly growing. Men usually color their hair to either hide gray hair or to make a fashion statement. Either way, you will look different than you did the day before.

Hair shafts are covered with a cuticle. Inside the cuticle is melanin, which accounts for the color of your hair. Coloring hair is a two-part process. In the first part, the cuticle must swell and crack to let the color in. The melanin inside your hair can then be either bleached or darkened.

Let's go to a darker color first. The hair dye stains the existing melanin and creates large, complex molecules. After a length of time, the excess dye chemicals are washed off leaving you with a new shade. The molecules inside the cuticle are now too big to easily wash out with shampoo, so your hair has a new color. Since everyone has different levels of melanin, they can end up with a slightly different hue even when they use the same chemical amounts.

To lighten hair, the cuticle must still be opened up to get inside the shaft. A bleaching agent, like hydrogen peroxide, removes some of the color of the melanin (or all of it depending on how long you leave it in). The new color combines with the melanin molecules to form the large molecules that won't wash out. With permanent hair color, your hair must grow out to replace the colored melanin. The secret to temporary colors is the size of the molecules. By making the colored molecules smaller, you can get them to shampoo out quicker. You can even spray paint your hair for Halloween—or to get a gig with a punk band.

HOW DO YOU KNOW IF SHE HATES YOUR GIFT?

Up to 90 percent of all communication is nonverbal, and her body language will tell you if she is upset with her gift. Her eyes sag a tiny bit, even if she is trying to save your feelings. Her smile involves only the mouth—the sign of a plastic, fake smile. True smiles light up the entire face. To see a true smile, surprise her with a diamond tennis bracelet for absolutely no reason. To see a fake smile, give her a vacuum cleaner on her fortieth birthday at a surprise party with your best friends. Psychology can be a wonderful branch of science, but it won't help you if you bought her a vacuum cleaner for a gift.

The problem is that guys don't read body language well. Committed guys learn to read their partner's body because of the time they spend together and the trial-and-error method. You screw up a trial and learn a little more about what each gesture means each time. We just need to learn to apply that body language intelligence beyond the house. Learning to read our coworkers would be a great skill. Salespeople either become very good at this or they find a new profession.

Body language may be the bulk of it, but guys love the spoken word. The spoken word can usually tell you if she likes your gift or not, but you have to notice the body language to be sure. If she opens the gift and repeats what it is, she hates it. For example, she opens a vacuum cleaner and says "Oh, a vacuum cleaner." You are in trouble.

There is an exception: If she repeats what the gift is while beaming a hundred-watt smile and jumping into your arms, you're safe. Jumping into your arms and planting a sexy kiss on you is not subtle. Remember, guys don't like subtlety. But we do like sexy kisses and hundred-watt smiles.

TEN: KITCHEN SCIENCE

Guys can cook; it just takes an open flame. This was a skill learned in the cowboy days. Gathered around the fire on a cattle trail, one guy had to be in charge of cooking. Picture a skinned rabbit on a spit above a fire, a pot of beans cooking in the coals, a cast-iron coffee pot, and you can feel the joy of cooking. Modern guys still love to cook over the open flame, but today it takes a stainless steel gas grill, a titanium barbecue tool set, and an apron that says "Danger, Men Cooking" to complete the meal.

Many men are grilling snobs. They can debate the advantages of briquettes, mesquite chips, and dry rubs for hours. Whether you are a snob or just an ordinary griller, the people you feed are going to be happy. Food just tastes better when it has been grilled to a delicate shade of black over an open fire.

Even beyond grilling, most of us are fascinated by food. I have a close female friend who says she would prefer to take a pill to eating. You will *never* hear a guy say that, never. We love to eat and we like to joke about food, with fruitcakes taking special abuse. We probably all have a favorite food cooked by a treasured relative. We watch in fascination as a little guy wolfs down sixty hot dogs, but few of us appreciate the science behind food. So turn up the flame as we examine the wonderful world of food science.

WHAT IS THE BEST WAY TO AVOID WATERY MUSTARD?

While men love food, there is one thing that annoys us—watery mustard. Many a good hot dog bun has been ruined by that initial squirt of yellow water. Of course, a good shake will clear up most of the problem, but it is hard to remember that every time. A better tactic in group settings is to let someone else enjoy that watery squirt. Offer the bottle to someone else first, then use the bottle next. Another way is to avoid squeeze bottles for mustard. Buy jars instead, because you'll always remember to stir when you see the layer of water on top when you open it up.

Mustard is usually made from ground mustard seeds, water, vinegar, and other spices. The ground mustard seeds will settle to the bottom of the jar, and it will take a really good shake to completely mix the seed parts. You can buy dry mustard and make it yourself, but it will still end up watery until stirred. A better option is pub mustard. Pub mustard trades water for beer—brilliant! I don't think men would ever complain about a little squirt of beer. My hat is off to the English (or Irish) inventors of pub mustard.

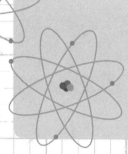

HOW DOES POPCORN POP?

Most of us enjoy the great smell and taste of hot popcorn, but how does it pop? The not-so-secret ingredient is water. Each kernel contains 12–15 percent water mixed in with the starchy corn endosperm. Endosperm is the starchy nutrient in most seeds. Wheat endosperm is ground up to make flour. If the whole-wheat kernel is used, it's called whole-wheat flour. White bread is made from pure wheat endosperm. The outer skin of popcorn (called the pericarp) is much tougher than traditional corn. As you heat the kernel, the water expands as it vaporizes. The pressure created inside is phenomenal. When the pressure from the steam is large enough, the pericarp splits and you have popped corn.

The starchy endosperm expands as it pops open and reveals the soft, white starch that we love to eat. Nobody knows who first discovered popcorn, but it has been around for hundreds of years. Most of us are glad that some ancient civilization threw a few of the hard kernels into the fire. Movie theater owners are ecstatic that popcorn exists, since they make us reach deep into our wallets for that beloved white treat.

Scientifically Speaking

The microwave oven is the consolation prize for trying to understand physics.

—Jason Love

HOW DO MICROWAVE OVENS WORK?

Microwave ovens have allowed men to fend for themselves with hot food. No more endless bologna sandwiches and burnt pots trying to cook mac-n-cheese. And we owe it all to a melted candy bar. The heart of a microwave oven is the magnetron. When experimenting with magnetrons for radar waves to help develop radar, Dr. Percy Spencer realized that the candy bar in his pocket melted when he stood in a certain place. Intrigued, the next day he brought in popcorn and aimed the magnetron at the popcorn. Percy was rewarded with a snack. He later tried an egg with explosive results. Millions of men rejoiced because we could finally cook our own hot meals, and millions of teenagers zapped eggs until they exploded.

Just like early television sets, the first microwave ovens were the size of a refrigerator. Advances in electronics led to the smaller ovens we use today.

"Nuked" and "zapped" are exaggerations when describing how a microwave works. Microwaves—electromagnetic waves similar to visible light, radio waves, and X-rays—are not dangerous to anything but water molecules and then only if they are focused. Water molecules are polar, which means one end is positive and the other end is negative. The microwaves cause these polar molecules to rotate as the waves pass through. The molecules try to line up with the microwave as it passes through the food.

Did You Know?

You can make a grape spark in a microwave oven. Using a sharp knife, slice the grape down the center leaving only a small strip connecting the two halves of the grape. Spread the grape open in the microwave. Microwave on high and watch the sparks.

You can think of it like bobbing in the waves on a surf-board. The water rotates as the waves go by. This rotating of water causes the temperature to rise and your food to get hot. Since the waves are focused in certain areas, a rotating table helps to get all of the food relatively hot. Some microwave ovens also use a fan to stir the waves; otherwise, only certain areas would get cooked.

How a Microwave Oven Works

The water molecule is polar and rotates as the microwave goes through it. The food heats up because the molecules are moving faster.

WHY DON'T FROZEN HOT DOGS COOK IN A MICROWAVE OVEN?

Frozen hot dogs do cook, but not very well. Pop one into a microwave oven and you will learn more about water and microwaves. One part of the hot dog will remain frozen while another part overheats and explodes open. The secret to exploding hot dogs is in the water, not in the microwave. Frozen water (better known as ice) locks the water molecules in a lattice structure, and the molecules just aren't as free to jiggle. The waves add energy, and a few start to break free from their chains. These free water molecules heat up rapidly while many frozen ones stay frozen. The free molecules eventually become so excited they blow a hole in the side of your hot dog. You end up with exploded hot dog goop only inches from a frozen part. To help solve this problem, microwave ovens usually have a defrost cycle for frozen food. The magnetron turns off for short periods of time to allow heat from the thawed parts to melt more ice. Heat will then transfer to melt the ice before the magnetron kicks back into gear.

Thawing meat is one of the better uses for a microwave oven. Pull out some chicken and you can be grilling in ten minutes. Your mom may have left food out on the counter to thaw in the good old days, but not anymore. If thawing on the countertop is a no-no, I have one question for you: Are you alive? I don't remember any kid dying in school from eating counter-thawed meat. Just as I thought, it didn't kill you either. Luckily we have the microwave oven; we can thaw meat and keep the experts happy at the same time.

Scientifically Speaking

In my house, we obey the law of thermodynamics.

—Homer Simpson

WHY IS THERE A METAL RACK IN YOUR MICROWAVE?

Many of us have started a fire by accidentally microwaving a piece of metal. And maybe even a few of us started a fire on purpose using a piece of metal. Not me, Mom, I swear it was an accident! Metal pieces start fires, so how come my oven has a metal rack? And come to think of it, doesn't my microwave oven have a metal shell? And doesn't my Hot Pocket have a metal sleeve?

The metal shell of the microwave oven actually helps the cooking process along, and the walls reflect the microwaves. The electromagnetic microwave causes free charges in the metal wall to accelerate and absorb the original microwaves. As these charges accelerate, they emit new microwaves back into the oven. So the waves essentially bounce off the walls back to the food. Even the metal screen covering the glass window does the same thing. The openings of the screen are so small the microwaves can't get through and are reflected back inside. Typical microwaves have a wavelength of twelve centimeters, and each screen opening is only a few millimeters.

The problem with metal in the microwave oven comes from sharp points like those on aluminum foil and twist ties. If enough of the free charges pile up at points on a metal surface, they will jump off into the air. Spark!

This spark can then ignite something else and you have fire. Never put sharp metal objects in a microwave, unless you want a light show.

Microwave ovens don't brown food since they cook from the inside out. Hot Pockets and other guy foods actually come with metal sleeves or trays to help them cook. The sleeve has just enough metal in it to allow the free charges inside it to move and heat up. This process is similar to when thin strips of metal heat up in an incandescent light bulb, and it is called resistive heating. This allows more heat on the surface of the food that will cause it to brown (a little) and become crisp.

Brain Fart

Microwave ovens were designed for guys. They deliver quick, hot food and the occasional fire. What's not to love?

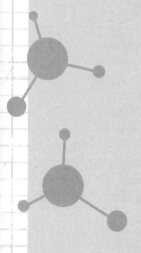

WHERE DO BEER STREAMERS COME FROM?

Beer is a lovely liquid that gives many men the ability to dance, or at least try. Beer also offers several lessons in science. Pour beer into a glass and watch the bubbles form. The bubbles form beer streamers, tiny rising rivers of bubbles that originate from a few points inside the glass. Their mesmerizing dance as they rise to the surface captures our attention. What causes them and why do they rise?

The bubbles are formed when carbon dioxide molecules begin to form invisible microbubbles at imperfections (or possibly at dirt particles inside the glass) on the inside wall of the glass, called nucleation points. Once enough of these microbubbles join forces, they begin their hypnotic rise to the surface. The bubbles actually grow in size as they rise since the pressure from the liquid decreases and will cease when the beer becomes flat. And, of course, the bubbles rise because they are gas, which is less dense than the liquid. The same observation can be seen in champagne and in clear sodas. The formation of these bubbles is similar to clouds forming by water vapor condensing around dust particles.

An interesting note: Beer bubbles rise slower than champagne bubbles. Leonardo da Vinci (1452–1519) first explored this concept as he studied bubbles rising in various liquids. The study of beer bubbles would be a perfectly reasonable graduate-school topic. I mean if Leonardo could get away with it, we ought to be able to.

HOW DO TURKEY THERMOMETERS KNOW WHEN TO POP UP?

Turkey is a holiday staple in many households. Most of us just head to the table while Mom cooks away. The secret to a safe bird is getting the meat temperature to at least 85°C (185°F). The pop-up timer is a foolproof method to ensure that happens. Serious cooks just pull out the plastic devices, but novices love the convenience.

The pop-up timer is similar to a spring-loaded plastic syringe. The end of the plunger is embedded in a piece of metal when the spring is compressed. The metal melts at 85°C, and the spring pops up, letting us know the bird is cooked. The timers can actually be reused by compressing the spring and dipping the end in boiling water. Hold it until the metal cools and it will be ready to go again.

> ### Did You Know?
> Ben Franklin stunned himself while trying to electrocute a turkey in 1750. He thought a jolt of electricity would make the bird more tender.

Of course, men have figured out a way to get into the turkey fun by deep-frying the poor bird. The timers are supposed to even work when the bird is fried, or so the maker claims. The timers were actually invented by the same man who patented the wire torture device used to keep the drumsticks in place while the bird sizzles. Would the timer work in Tofurkey? Would it work on a turducken? On your next turkey holiday you can ponder this question as you eat 5,000 calories of food.

WHAT CAUSES ICE CREAM HEADACHES (BRAIN FREEZE)?

A hot summer day and a bowl of ice cream just go together. To combat the heat, you take a large bite. It tastes good, but here comes the pain, a stabbing pain that causes temporary insanity. You want to scream as your forehead throbs, but then it disappears as fast as it showed up. So you go right back to the spoon for more.

Most of us know this experience as a brain freeze, and the pain is excruciating. But is your brain really freezing? No, it is just fooled into being cold. Run your tongue along the roof of your mouth and you'll feel a bump. The area behind that bump is responsible for the brain freeze. Directly above this area is a collection of nerves that feed into your brain.

Eating ice cream or drinking a Slurpee too fast causes these nerves to get cold. Your brain dilates the blood vessels to deliver extra warm blood to "thaw out" your brain. This extra blood flow leads to the debilitating pain you experience. It goes away after twenty to thirty seconds, but it can bring you to your knees while present.

You can get rid of brain freeze by pressing your tongue against the roof of your mouth. Your tongue warms up the nerves and slows down the rush of blood. You can completely avoid ice cream headaches by eating more slowly. Letting the ice cream melt more in the front of your mouth also works. You could also just avoid eating ice cream altogether . . . nope, didn't think so. Many of us avoid Slurpees after the age of fifteen, but I am not sure why.

Ice cream headaches only occur in about one-third of the population, so some people are lucky. I suffer and will continue to do so. My food pyramid is stacked on top of an ice cream bowl. If I ever get arrested, I am going to try the ice cream headache defense to get off.

Scientifically Speaking

Science is always wrong. It never solves a problem without creating ten more.

—George Bernard Shaw

CAN BEER BATTERIES SAVE THE WORLD'S OIL SUPPLY?

The beer battery, or getting electricity from beer, sounds like a great concept. Of course, many people would argue that beer is more important than electricity. However, you will be pleased to find out that beer batteries don't waste any beer. They are just a cute name for a microbial fuel cell (MFC). *Beer battery* became the accepted name after Foster's Group brewery and Queensland University combined forces to work on MFCs, which use the wastewater left from the beer-making process to create electricity. You get beer and electricity!

> ## Brain Fart
> Support bacteria, it's the only culture some people have.

MFCs use bacteria to break down the alcohol, sugar, and starches that are left over from the brewing process. After the bacteria goes to work, you are left with electricity, clean water, and carbon dioxide. This process will work in most food and beverage creation processes. It's a great way to clean the wastewater, and you get a little electricity to boot.

The world definitely needs to do more research into MFCs. I feel confident many people would be willing to help drink the beer. More beer equals more wastewater and more electricity. So lift a pint to help the world. If we could just get science to work on the urine battery, then beer could possibly save the world's oil supply in the brewery and the bathroom.

WHY DO SNACK CAKES NEVER MOLD?

As a teacher, I once took a snack cake away from a student who was trying to eat it in class. I thought to myself, if I can't eat in class, no one can. I proceeded to make a joke about the whole thing and said we were going to create a science experiment. I placed the offending cake on the top ledge of my blackboard to observe over the next few days. Days turned into months. The unwrapped cake lasted from November until June with no mold growth. We had a class funeral for the cake before it met the trash can. The class offered me ten dollars to eat it. The thought tempted me, but I decided not to. After all, it wasn't a chocolate cake. The cream filling was still soft, even though the outside was a little tough.

Why don't snack cakes grow mold? I suspected that it had something to do with a lack of actual food, so I set out to investigate why. I invested in every snack cake on the market. The first thing I learned is that reading the ingredient list can only be accomplished with a PhD in chemistry looking over your shoulder. These things have more preservatives than your favorite old actress.

The number-one ingredient in most is enriched flour. Does taking ordinary flour and adding a multivitamin make these little cholesterol bombs healthy? Ingredients on a package are listed in order of amount. The first ingredient has the greatest percentage, the second listed ingredient has the second highest percentage, and so on. I say that because several of the next few ingredients are similar. Sugar is high on the list, which is to be expected; it is a snack cake, not a health food snack. Corn syrup is also high up on the list, and this is really just liquid sugar. Look farther and you will see high-fructose corn syrup, which is sugar with a higher sugar content. Put all of this together and you have a ton of sugar, flour, and multivitamins. And vitamins are good for you, so eat away.

The next dozen or so ingredients look like they could be found in a college chemistry class. Basically, they have taken anything that can spoil in the cake and replaced it with a chemical to keep it from going rancid. Sorbic acid is the only listed ingredient that actually is a preservative. If you look down near the bottom, you will see natural and artificial flavoring. I guess natural flavorings weren't good enough, so they threw in some artificial.

People today live longer than they did one hundred years ago. Maybe it is due to advances in medicine, but I have my own completely unscientific theory. I think people live longer because of Twinkies and white bread. By the age of twenty, we have eaten enough preservatives to add twenty years to our lives. I am also not even sure funeral parlors need to embalm people anymore. Many of us have already embalmed ourselves with Ho-Hos and Swiss Cake Rolls. Maybe Hollywood stars just need more snack cakes to fight off the ravages of age. Of course, they wouldn't age at all if they were hermetically sealed in a plastic pouch like a snack cake.

Did You Know?

A baker named James Dewar came up with the name "Twinkie" when driving by a billboard for the Twinkle Toe Shoe Company.

WHAT IS THE SECRET TO WINNING A HOT DOG EATING CONTEST?

Many of us have no urge to eat seventy-two hot dogs in five minutes, but we are still fascinated by people who can. These fun contests are covered by ESPN and all of the cable news networks.

I was the every Friday cheese grit eating champion of Brentwood Elementary but never did any formal training. I could have had a future if I had been more dedicated, or if I had a really cool nickname. Unlike me, competitive eaters actually train for these events. They exercise like madmen and do things to purposefully distend their stomachs like drinking gallons of water in very short periods of time to stretch the stomach. Competitive eaters also have their own organization, the International Federation of Competitive Eaters. It is the national governing board of gluttony and keeps records and world rankings.

Just the simple joy of eating is elevated to a new level in these displays of gluttony. Hot dogs get the most press, but all manner of foods are competed over. Wings, shrimp, asparagus, and ramen noodles are all big-time contests. My friends and I had a better food contest in college. When we went out to hoist a few brews, the last one to "break the seal" (go wee-wee) was a winner. This person didn't get a trophy or a check, only our admiration. As all guys know, after you break the seal you will have to go every three minutes if you continue to consume beer.

Competitive hot dog eaters all appear to use the same technique. First they take the dog out of the bun and fold the dog in half. The entire dog is shoved into the mouth and swallowed. The bun is then dipped in water and crammed into the cheek to be swallowed as they break another dog. The stomach is an amazing organ; it can expand to up to fifty times its empty volume. As us mortals eat too much, we get sick and our stomachs hurt. Trained eaters know how to deal with this unpleasantness. They get comfortable with that "my stomach is full of seventy-two hot dogs" feeling. After all, they have to be able to smile as they are handed the award check. Then it is off to the restroom to purge. I am glad they don't televise that part of the contest.

Brain Fart

Competitive eaters can retire to pro wrestling after their gluttonous days are over—they already have cool nicknames.

WHY DO ONIONS MAKE YOU CRY?

If you cut onions, you will cry like you just watched a chick flick. What? Don't all guys cry at chick flicks? The secret to onion tears is battery acid (aka sulfuric acid). We would never purposely put battery acid in our eyes, but when you slice through an onion, you open up cells and allow all of the stuff inside to mix, mainly enzymes and sulfur-containing compounds. After a few chemical reactions, they form a volatile gas that drifts skyward.

When this volatile gas reaches the moisture in your eye it forms battery acid. Your eyes then produce more water (tears) to dilute the battery acid. Your eyes are irritated by the acid so you rub them. Of course, your fingers are covered with more of the offending chemicals so you cry more. It can turn into a regular sobfest if you aren't careful. Most of us haven't cried that hard since the Red Sox finally won a World Series.

This begs the question, how do you stop the tears when cutting onions? Wear goggles. You can look cool and cut the onions at the same time! Actually, you could just cut the onion under a stream of cold water. Since the chemicals are water soluble they will just run down the drain. This gives an added benefit of washing the blood down the drain when you slice into your thumb. Putting the onion in the freezer for ten minutes before cutting will also slow down the reaction.

Another method that works well is chewing on the end of a match as you cut. This is perfect for large groups since you will look macho on two fronts. One, the match looks cool, and two, you don't cry when you slice into the offending orb. The sulfur compound on the match head helps to neutralize the gas. You can also chew gum, but the match just looks cooler.

DO PIGS HAVE
SPARE RIBS?

Not if you ask the pig. The pig is probably quite attached to all of his ribs. They aren't like lizard tails, which grow back. The only way to get the spareribs is to remove them, and, trust me, they don't send boneless pigs back into the sty. We just don't think about the term as we head to a barbecue joint.

A barbecue fan would definitely say the pig has no spare ribs. Matter of fact, to a fan, the pig has no spare parts, only parts to be smoked, barbecued, pulled, sliced, diced, and eaten. The meat industry doesn't even try to disguise what happens to pigs. You can look no further than the terms *baby back ribs* and *whole-hog sausage*. I wonder where they come from . . .

Spareribs are actually the normal rib cage of the hog, not really spare at all. Baby back ribs are not from junior pigs but are actually smaller ribs found near the backbone of the pig. A favorite of many barbecue fans is the Boston butt, which isn't a butt at all. It actually comes from the top of the front shoulder of the pig. Hams come from the back legs, although shoulder hams come from the lower front leg. Bacon usually comes from the belly of the pig and contains plenty of fat. And fatback (a Southern staple for seasoning) is just the fat along the backbone. Whole-hog sausage should really be called almost-whole-hog sausage, since they normally don't use the head or the feet. Just put all the parts through a grinder and add some spices. Useful meat in the head is used to create headcheese (brawn in the U.K.). The feet get pickled for us to gnaw on. Are you hungry yet?

ELEVEN: THE BIG THREE

The manliest things in the universe are duct tape, silicon spray (WD-40), and the remote control. In the manliness pantheon, these three sit at the right hand of fire. For men, fire is number one, but these three fall closely behind. Man-inventions invented for men by men; it just doesn't get any manlier.

Duct tape and silicon spray allow you to fix anything. If something is stuck and you want it unstuck, just use silicon spray. If it isn't stuck and you want it stuck, just use duct tape. These two inventions allow any man to improvise on the fly. No job is too tough with these two in your arsenal.

The remote control is definitely a guy thing. In the old days, a remote wasn't needed. You had three channels and a dial knob. With the advent of cable and satellite, a remote is essential. No longer do we need to watch commercials or anything that bores us within twelve seconds. Two hundred channels and you still may find nothing to watch, but you get to enjoy the ride. In the dark ages of three channels, we always wondered if we were missing something good on another channel. With a remote control and two hundred channels, we know that we won't miss anything.

Let's examine the science behind the big three. How do remote controls work? How many remotes does a guy need to feel manly? Why does duct tape rule the adhesive market? How did WD-40 get its name? What happens if you spray duct tape with silicon spray? Grab a seat in your easy chair as we examine the manliest three inventions on the planet.

HOW DO IR REMOTE CONTROLS WORK?

Throughout history, wars have contributed mightily to the knowledge leading to man-inventions. Remotes were developed to help the military explode bombs and reroute ships. After the fighting ceased, intrepid scientists tried to find better ways to use this knowledge. Remotely exploding a bomb is a tad violent, but changing the channel on my TV is completely safe. Out of the ashes of warfare arose one of the ultimate cool man tools.

The most basic television remotes use infrared (IR) light. Infrared is a portion of the electromagnetic spectrum just outside of visible light. Inside the remote control you have electrical contacts that correspond to your touch pad. Pressing a button sends a signal to the microprocessor of the remote. The microprocessor then sends a binary code—a series of ones and zeroes—to the light-emitting diode (LED) on the end of the remote. Every command has a different binary signal that contains a code for the particular device and then a series of ones and zeroes that correspond to the desired action. It then finishes off with an end code for the device. The light essentially flashes on and off rapidly (and in the correct sequence). A receiver on the front of the television picks up the flashing light, and the signal is relayed to the television's microprocessor. You can't see the flashing light because IR is invisible to our eye. Even if you could see it, the flashes are too fast for your eye to detect. You get to surf, change the volume, and mute the TV, all at the push of a button.

IR remotes have a few downsides. One, they are basically line of sight. A stronger LED will allow the aim to be off a little, but the TV's eye still needs to see the signal. Second, interference from other IR sources has to be limited. You can accomplish this in a couple of ways. The remote uses only one frequency of light, and the TV can only accept the same frequency. Also, watching TV indoors is a good idea, since the sun gives off IR waves, and IR remotes are limited to about ten meters of effective range.

The IR remote is the old standard, but remote technology is getting better. I look forward to the day where we won't even need to push buttons; my thumb gets tired easily. We will just think about changing the channel and our television will start scanning the airwaves. When we reach that level, watching TV with your hyperactive best friend would be really fun.

Brain Fart

Infrared waves not only help your remote control, they also keep sandwiches warm for days at a time at your favorite fast-food restaurant.

HOW DO RF REMOTE
CONTROLS WORK?

Radio frequency (RF) remotes are the second-most-popular type. Key fobs, garage door openers, and remote control toys all use RF remotes. RF remotes use a radio frequency to deliver the signal. After that, they work essentially the same as the IR remotes with one big advantage: range.

RF remotes have an effective range of about thirty yards. The signal will also go around corners and through walls. Since they aren't line of sight, you don't have to lift your arm at weird angles to get the device to work. Many high-end audiovisual components now come with RF remotes.

Garage door remotes and key fobs are now sending a coded signal to deter thieves. In the old days, you could drive around the neighborhood and probably open several other doors with your remote garage door opener. The codes are scrambled now, and only the correct transmitter can activate the opener.

Key fobs are also more user-friendly today. I drive one of the most unmanly cars on the planet: a white minivan. Do you know how many white vans are on the road? On any given Saturday in a mall parking lot you might see a thousand. Luckily, one press of the button and my car lights flash and the doors open. I haven't lost my car yet, and the door is always unlocked waiting for me. If we had bought the deluxe van, I wouldn't even have to open the door with my hand at all. Another press of the button and the door would magically open.

Scientifically Speaking

Genius is one percent inspiration and ninety-nine percent perspiration.

—Thomas Edison

WHAT IS THE BEST TYPE OF REMOTE IN THE UNIVERSE?

Universal remote controls give you the ability to control everything in your life. For a few years they were the playground of the rich, but not anymore. Gone are the days of a coffee table full of remote controls. It used to take my best friend six minutes to play a CD because of the twelve remotes that all had to be used in the correct sequence. It was probably easier to launch a nuclear missile than to hear music at his house.

New remotes also have learning capabilities. You just aim another remote at the new one, and the new one will learn all of the codes for each desired feature. It will take a few days to program, but it beats having twelve different remotes. Universal remotes can be either IR or RF style remotes. The technology is the same; universal remotes just have more buttons.

Many universal remotes now come with LCD touchpads to make surfing easier. Touching the pad causes the circuit to be complete, and the signal is sent to the correct toy (oops, electrical component). They are easier to see in the dark because the pad is lit, and they are a great way to make your guy friends envious. Of course, first dates may think you are a technogeek and never want to see you again, but dating another technogeek is a great option. They are impressed with your toys and almost always make great money.

Now if they could just put a beeper on the remote so you won't lose it. Even universal remotes are still going to slip into the couch. Maybe we need scientists to get to work on the brain-driven remote control. If you are a scientist, put down this book and go to work. *Now*!

HOW DO MOTION-ACTIVATED HANDHELD VIDEO GAME CONTROLLERS WORK?

Handheld game controllers are going to continue to change the way we play our video games. They are already changing game play and draining our wallets at astounding speed. No longer is moving the control around just a silly looking part of the game; it is now required. Keeping up with game technology is difficult because it grows by leaps and bounds yearly. The big three video game companies are always searching for new ways to drain our wallets, but we gladly comply. The only guarantee is that next year there will be a better game system.

Motion-activated game controllers are going to govern the next few revolutions in game play. We'll take a look at how the Wii controller works first. The Wii is the first game to make the controller the star attraction, although more are sure to follow. By the time you read this a new one will probably be reaching into your wallet, but it will owe its start to the Wii.

> ### Brain Fart
>
> The next generation of video games may actually involve being shot and killed by your own computer.

The Wii controller makes use of two different technologies. First, it uses a standard infrared signal to generate position of the controller. A sensor bar is mounted on the top or bottom of the television screen. The bar sends an IR signal from each end toward your controller. Knowing where those two beams intersect will give the console the location of the remote. Think of it as a triangle. The sensor bar is fixed and shoots two beams, which cross at the front of the controller. This location is fed back into the processor that drives the game.

Second, the controllers use tiny microelectromechanical system (MEMS) accelerometers. Accelerometers measure acceleration. Acceleration is directly related to force, and these MEMS are the heart of the controller. These three-axis MEMS can determine the force (and angle) of the controller through the use of a tiny mass suspended on even tinier springs. As you move the controller, the mass inside will move. By measuring the acceleration of the movement, the processor determines force. The angle is determined by the three degrees of movement.

Of course, you also have to press buttons at the correct time, just like in the good old days. The processor puts the position, angle, button controls, and force together and compares them to preprogrammed motions to tell you if your movement was any good. This same technology works for any game you are playing. The future of video games will take us farther down this road.

We sure have come a long way from Pong. My brother and I had to sit next to each other as we tried to achieve Pong domination. You had to spin a dial knob mounted on the console, which was the size of a shoebox. Then we progressed to games of three-man football with a square football. Today, by adding new technologies into the mix, new consoles continue to amaze us. When you have kids, you'll be forced to stand in line to buy the newest console because "Billy has one." "Billy has one" is the preteen equivalent of keeping up with the Joneses. As adults, we don't like being deprived of cool toys, and neither do our kids. Today's video games are actually a great way to bond with our families; we can even get exercise as we play video games now. Honestly though, sometimes I miss the square football.

WHY IS DUCK/DUCT TAPE GREAT?

Duck tape is the tape of choice for all intrepid guys. A single roll can clear a honey-do list faster than anything. All men should have a roll in the house and one in the car. Duck tape is the waterproof cousin of white athletic tape. Both of these should be staples in all men's houses. If you are a new dad, a roll of the white tape is a must in the diaper bag. There is quite a bit of disagreement over the name and origin of duck tape, but either way, men are glad it was invented.

It is commonly thought that duck tape was originally developed by the Johnson & Johnson Company during World War II to seal ammunition boxes. This makes sense, since duck tape is just a waterproof version of the medical tape J&J was already supplying to the military. The dispute over the real name is a little more complicated.

The name is thought to come from one of two sources. One, since it was waterproof, the water rolls off it like off a duck's back. Or two, the cloth part of the tape is made of cotton duck. Either way, the GIs soon found out that it was good for a million different uses. The term *duct tape* shows up later when it was used to seal air-conditioning ducts. The name Duck Tape was trademarked in the 1980s by a company that specializes in the tape (not J&J).

What makes it so great? The tape is composed of three layers. The inner layer is a rubber-based adhesive. The middle is the fabric cloth that lends

Scientifically Speaking

Magnetism is one of the Six Fundamental Forces of the Universe, with the other five being Gravity, Duct Tape, Whining, Remote Control, and The Force That Pulls Dogs Toward The Groins Of Strangers.

—Dave Barry

strength and allows the tape to tear easily. The outside is a waterproof vinyl now available in a multitude of colors, although actual duct tape is a bright silver color. Waterproof, tough, and easy to tear makes duck tape a winner in the guy world. There are tapes that do each trait better than duck tape, but not a single tape that is more versatile.

Duck tape has legions of adoring fans. It has been used to make prom dresses, wedding tuxedoes, and in a million other unique ways. Entire books have been written to pay homage to that crazy tape. Duck tape or duct tape—either way, men love it. I am pretty sure somewhere in the annals of history an actual duck was taped with duck tape, but I have not been able to find any credible research on the subject. It has to work; duck tape sticks to everything. If you see a silver-coated duck walking around town, you will know that I was just doing some research. No actual ducks were harmed in the making of this book.

HOW DOES WD-40 WORK?

WD-40 has been a staple of households for years, and the blue and yellow can has ended more squeaks than anything in the history of civilization. One spray and the creaks are gone. Things just move easier under the influence of WD-40. Duck tape and WD-40 have been called the redneck repair kit, but every man needs a can and a roll to make his life complete.

Mix a little aliphatic hydrocarbons, petroleum oil, carbon dioxide, and a few other ingredients together and you have WD-40. Aliphatic hydrocarbons are long, straight-chained hydrocarbons. These hydrocarbons are flammable (as any WD-40 fan will tell you). These hydrocarbons are in the same family as wax, so they are a successful lubricant. Carbon dioxide is the primary propellant used to launch that great liquid out of the can. Petroleum oil is pretty much the same as the good old-fashioned penetrating oil that your grandpa used. Of course, since 1958 he probably used WD-40.

> **Did You Know?**
>
> WD-40 has been used to remove a boa constrictor from a car engine, lubricate inner tubes for sledding, and clean prosthetic limbs.

WD-40 stands for Water Displacement perfected on the fortieth try. I for one am glad that it was finished on the fortieth try; WD-38 just doesn't roll off the tongue. Originally designed by the Rocket Chemical Company—which actually changed their name to the WD-40 Company—it was designed as a rust-prevention solvent for the aerospace industry and was used on the Atlas missile to stop corrosion and rust. It worked for that but also found a million other uses. Many of the engineers snuck cans home to fix all manner of problems. In 1958, the company started selling it to the public and a legend was born. The secret formula is still in use today. A few brand names have been added to the WD-40 Company brand family over the years, but WD-40 will always be near and dear to the male heart.

Fixing squeaky hinges, removing tar, loosening nuts, and preventing rust are a few of the most common uses, but intrepid men have developed thousands of other uses for that yellow and blue can. My favorite is fuel for a spud gun, but many uses are safer. Removing crayon marks from all manners of stuff is a great use for a new dad. I also like spraying the top of my birdfeeder, so squirrels just slide off. For you gamblers out there, it also cleans dice and pool cues. However, there is no proof that is a cure-all for arthritis. I don't think spraying it on your knee is going to lubricate your joints.

That familiar blue and yellow can is a staple of manhood. A can for the garage is pretty much guaranteed to make your life easier. Ask your friends for their favorite uses; they are going to surprise you. If you want something to move, just grab that can. A can also makes the perfect gift idea for any manly man. My dad is hard to buy for, so last year I got him a can of WD-40 and a roll of duct tape. It was the best present he opened and two gifts he is sure to use.

WHAT HAPPENS IF YOU SPRAY DUCT TAPE WITH WD-40?

The space-time continuum is based on the assumption that everything can be described by four dimensions. Length, width, and height will give you the where, and time, the fourth dimension, will give you the when. You can only be in any one place at one time in your life. We use the space-time continuum every time we make plans with our friends. We agree on a time and a physical location—four dimensions! If you get the day wrong, you may be by yourself.

In our everyday life, time is constant, but as an object approaches the speed of light, time, length, and even mass change. Wow! Time takes on a new meaning since it is related to velocity. Einstein garnered most of his fame dealing with this thought, although the crazy hair helped his celebrity. If he were bald, he probably wouldn't have been famous. Experiments have proved his theory to be correct. The space-time continuum also shows up in virtually every sci-fi book or movie. The continuum lends itself so well to time travel. Ten thousand years ago, where you sit now might have been underwater. In books and movies, you can travel back in time and make small changes that impact tons of future decisions. We love it and we go along for the ride.

WD-40 and duct tape are complete opposites. No mixing of these two is allowed. In a simple world, spraying WD-40 onto duct tape would just

Scientifically Speaking

Space isn't remote at all. It's only an hour's drive away if your car could go straight upwards.

—Fred Hoyle

cancel both out. Think of it as eating ice cream while jogging on a treadmill, but in man land it is more complicated.

I have my own private, nonscientific theory. Mixing the two is like seeing yourself during time travel—guaranteed to destroy the universe. The initial spray onto the duct tape will appear normal, but rapidly you will rip holes in the space-time continuum. The spray would create a mini black hole. Time slows down as it nears the warped space created by a black hole. The black hole would slowly pull nearby objects in. As you are pulled into the black hole, you would be spaghettified as the intense gravity stretches you out.

Please, for the sake of humanity, never spray duct tape with WD-40. Our world may have issues, but we don't want to destroy it. I recommend storing duct tape and WD-40 in separate locations in your house to minimize the chances of an accidental rip in the continuum. Of course, maybe spraying WD-40 on duct tape won't do anything, but is it really worth taking the chance?

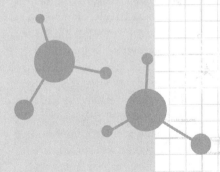

WHY ARE WARS GOOD
FOR SCIENCE?

Wars do more to help technology than most peacetime research has ever done. This is sad but true. During times of war, we dedicate vast sums of money and brainpower into focused pursuits. Of course, most of these pursuits are designed to give us a leg up on the enemy, which is a politically correct term for better ways to kill people.

Nuclear power, microwave ovens, remote controls, duct tape, and WD-40 are just a few things either invented in times of war or devices that grew out of wartime research. WD-40 grew out of the Cold War, a war that involved no killing but tons of new technology. The arms race was a boon to guys. We got tons of new guy toys with no loss of life, a win-win situation. Of course, the space race also developed tons of new toys, so maybe it ranks with the Cold War. Most problems in the world can be solved if we focus our money and brains on them.

Many of the same wonderful guy toys may also be our downfall. Is the next Isaac Newton spending twenty-two hours a day trying to conquer the next video game craze? Is the next Lonnie Johnson too busy to invent because he is watching *Spider-Man 7* in his home theater for the ninety-second time?

Maybe playing with guy toys will lead us to new ways to improve the world. Hopefully we will never stop inventing, discovering, and playing. Out of this playtime will come new things to amuse us (and a sequel to this book).

Scientifically Speaking

Innocence about science is the worst crime today.

—Sir Charles Percy Snow

RESOURCES

About.com: Chemisty
www.chemistry.about.com

American Dental Association
www.ada.com

BaseballEquipment.com
www.baseballequipment.com

ConsumerAffairs.com
www.consumeraffairs.com

Helium
www.helium.com

Inquiry Journal
www.unh.edu/inquiryjournal

Live Science
www.livescience.com

Louisville Slugger Museum and Factory
www.sluggermuseum.org

National Hot Rod Association
www.nhra.com

Science Museum of Minnesota
www.smm.org

The Kitchen Project
www.kitchenproject.com

United States Golf Association
www.usga.org

WD-40 Company
www.wd40.com/uses

INDEX

A

Accelerometers, 205
ACHOO syndrome, 81
Active-matrix displays, 93
Adenosine triphosphate, 86
Air
    dams, 27
    pressure, 113
Airbag, 36-37
Alcohol
    blood alcohol content, 120
    and ice, 108
    and freezing, 122
    layered drinks, 109
    proof number, 109
    tricks, 113, 114
Alligator, outrunning, 150-52
Animals, 145-63
Antilock brakes (ABS), 34

B

Baby back ribs, 197
Bacon, 197
Baffles, 142
Baseball
    curve, 52-53
    knuckleball, 54

Bats
    aluminum and distance, 64-65
    composite, 64-65
Beer
    batteries, 191
    can, crushing, 110
    freezing of, 123-24
    funnels, 116-17
    streamers, 187
Bernoulli effect, 52, 53, 130
Blasting cap, 3
Blood alcohol content (BAC), 120
Blowback, 22
Body
    functions, 67-87
    language, 177
Boston butt, 197
Bowling ball, 66
Brain freeze, 189-90
Brindley, Giles, 75
Building, implosion, 7-8
Buoyancy, 106
Brainwashing, 171
Breathalyzers, 120-21
    color change, 120-21
    fuel cell, 120, 121
    infrared spectroscopy, 120, 121

ABOUT THE AUTHOR

Bobby Mercer is an award-winning teacher, coach, author, and dad. He is the author of *Quarterback Dad: A Play-by-Play Guide to Tackling Your New Baby*, a fun look at fatherhood using American football terms. He has a science education degree from UCF and a master's degree in physics education from the University of Virginia. He is also the author of two juvenile science books: *Smash It! Crash It! Launch It!: 50 Mind-Blowing Eye-Popping Science Experiments* and *The Leaping, Sliding, Sprinting, Jumping Science Book: 50 Super Sports Science Activities*. He lives outside of Asheville, North Carolina, with his family (*www.bobbymercerbooks.com*).